A

NEW AND COMPREHENSIVE

GRAMMAR

OF THE

ENGLISH LANGUAGE

A

NEW AND COMPREHENSIVE

GRAMMAR

OF THE

ENGLISH LANGUAGE,

ARRANGED IN A POPULAR FORM,

WITH

NUMEROUS ANALYTICAL AND SYNTHETICAL ILLUSTRATIONS,

FOR THE

USE OF SCHOOLS AND PRIVATE INDIVIDUALS

BY

GEORGE KING

GYAN

Published by

Gyan Publishing House
5, Ansari Road
Daryaganj, New Delhi-110002
Phone: 011-47034999, 9811692060
E-mail: books@gyanbooks.com

Distribution Network
gyanbooks.com
India, USA, Canada, UK, Australia

ISBN: 978-93-6433-007-7 (PB)
First Published, 1854

2nd Impression 2024

Printed at: Gyan Press, Delhi.

A NEW AND COMPREHENSIVE GRAMMAR OF THE ENGLISH LANGUAGE
Author: GEORGE KING

A NEW AND COMPREHENSIVE GRAMMAR OF THE ENGLISH LANGUAGE,

ARRANGED IN A POPULAR FORM,

WITH

NUMEROUS ANALYTICAL AND SYNTHETICAL ILLUSTRATIONS,

FOR THE

USE OF SCHOOLS AND PRIVATE INDIVIDUALS,

BY

THE REV. GEORGE KING.

COVENTRY:

PUBLISHED BY G. R. AND F. W. KING, FLEET STREET;

LONDON: WHITTAKER AND CO., AVE MARIA LANE;
LAW, SCHOOL LIBRARY, 131, FLEET STREET.

TO BE HAD OF ALL BOOKSELLERS.

1854.

PREFACE.

The Author of the following Treatise on the English Language, in again submitting it to the public, feels encouraged by the many gratifying Testimonials he has received of its utility, and appropriate adaptation to the object it has in view.

He has, in many instances, forsaken the beaten path, as too rugged and devious, and chosen one which appears more easy and proximate to a thorough acquaintance with a Language which is now acquiring a kind of ubiquity on the habitable globe.

——— "Quis jam locus,—
"Quæ regio in terris nostri non plena laboris?"

Coventry, March, 1854.

ENGLISH GRAMMAR.

GRAMMAR instructs us in the analysis and composition of sentences.

English Grammar informs us of the English language in particular.

The English language is of Saxon origin, intermixed with derivations from the French, Latin, and Greek tongues.

It is now, perhaps, the most copious and eloquent of European languages.

English Grammar consists of four general divisions, viz.—ORTHOGRAPHY, ETYMOLOGY, SYNTAX, and PROSODY.

ORTHOGRAPHY.

ORTHOGRAPHY implies correct spelling; as such, it forms but a small part of a summary of Grammar.

Language is a combination of words, systematically arranged.

Words are composed of letters, and may consist of *one* syllable, as *eye*, *art*, *moss*, *straight;* or of *more* than *one*, as *art-ful*, *con-ju-gal*, *ef-fe-mi-nate*.

The letters of the Alphabet* are twenty-six in number, viz. *a*, *b*, *c*, *d*, *e*, *f*, *g*, *h*, *i*, *j*, *k*, *l*, *m*, *n*, *o*, *p*. *q*, *r*, *s*, *t*, *u*, *v*, *w*, *x*, *y*, *z*.

The letters consist of *vowels* and *consonants*.

The vowels are *a*, *e*, *i*, *o*, *u;* sometimes *y* is a vowel; then it is sounded like *i*.

---

* Alphabet is derived from the first two Greek letters, *alpha*, *beta*.

One or more of these vowels must be employed in the construction of every syllable

The remaining letters of the Alphabet are called *consonants*.

The vowels are simple sounds, and can be made by the tongue alone.

The consonants, as the name implies, are complex sounds, and in their utterance, the *lips*, the *teeth*, the *throat*, and the *palate* are required to assist the *tongue;* hence they are called, as they derive aid from these organs, *labials*, *dentals*, *gutturals*, and *palatals*. A few sounds derive assistance from the *nose*, and are hence termed *nasals*.

The letter *h* when sounded, is only a breathing, as in *heart*, *house*, *whet*, *rhetoric*, &c. It is then called *h aspirate*.

This letter is frequently *silent*, not breathed, as in *hour*, *heir*, *herb*, *honest*, &c. It is then termed *h mute*.

C and *g* have two sounds; the one *hard*, as in *cat*, *get;* the other *soft*, as in *city*, *gender*.

Letters are sounded together in *syllables;* a word derived from the Greek, and signifies *taking together*.

Words of *one* syllable are *monosyllables;*
Words of *two* syllables are *dissyllables;*
Words of *three* syllables are *trisyllables;*
Words of *many* syllables are *polysyllables*.

A good general rule for separating the syllables of a word, is to stop at the vowel, if only *one* consonant follows; as, *fe-li-ci-ty;* and to stop at the *former* consonant, when two consonants come together; as, *am-bas-sa-dor*. When an additional syllable is appended to a complete word, the best method is to terminate a syllable by the word; as, *con-tempt*, con-tempt-ible; *inform*, inform-a-tion; except when *gn* are the final letters; as, *benign*, be-nig-ni-ty.

A diphthong is the union of *two* vowels in *one* syllable, when *one* only is sounded, as *ea* in *eagle*; *ei* in *either*; *ie* in *believe*; or it is the combination of two vowels into one sound, as *oi* in *oil*; *ou* in *pound*; *ai* in *fair*.

A triphthong is the concurrence of *three* vowels in the *same* syllable, all pronounced as *one*, as *eau* in *beau*, *beauty*; *ieu* in *lieu*.

When two vowels in the same syllable take the sound of one only, it is called a *synœresis*, as *œ* in *œsophagus*; *ai* in *aisle*; *æ* in *Cæsar*; *eo* in *people*.

When two vowels in the same syllable are separately enunciated it is called a *Diæresis*, as *aërial*, *orthoëpy*. This mark (¨) diæresis is frequently placed over one of the vowels to designate such pronunciation.

There are other *marks* used in composition; of which the principal are here subjoined:

Hyphen (-); a mark used between compound words, as *luke-warm*; also at the end of a line, when only *part* of a word can be admitted, implying that the remaining part is in the next line.

Comma (,); the shortest stop in reading; a dash (—) is frequently substituted for a comma in epistolary compositions.

Semicolon (;); a stop somewhat longer than a *comma*, but not so long as a

Colon (:), which requires a more decided pause; and a

Period, or Full Stop (.) demands a complete suspension of the voice.

INTERROGATION (?) shews that a question is asked.

ADMIRATION, or EXCLAMATION (!) indicates some surprise or emotion of mind.

QUOTATION (" ")—This is used to shew that the words contained between the inverted and direct commas have been extracted from some author; as, Solomon says, "A wise son heareth his father's instruction."

It is not possible to reduce the Orthography of the English language to any fixed rules; a few general laws may, however, be advantageously introduced.

1. Monosyllables ending with *f*, *l*, or *s*, preceded by a single vowel, double those letters, as *stuff*, *call*, *kiss*. The exceptions to this rule are—*as*, *has*, *is*, *his*, *if*, *of*, *this*, *thus*, *was*, *us*, *yes*.

2. Monosyllables terminating in any consonant but *f*, *l*, or *s*, immediately after a single vowel, do not double the final letter, except—*add*, *butt*, *buzz*, *ebb*, *egg*, *err*, *inn*, *odd*, *purr*.

3. Words ending in *y* preceded by a *consonant*, change the *y* into *i*, on the addition of another syllable, except when *ing* or *ish* is added,* as bounty, bountiful.

But when the final *y* is preceded by a vowel, it remains unchanged, as *employ*, *employs*, *employment*, except *daily*, *gaily*, *laid*, *paid*, *said*.

4. Monosyllables, ending with a *single* consonant, preceded by a *single* vowel, double that consonant on the addition of another syllable, as *flit*, *flitting*; *thin*, *thinner*, *thinnest*.

Also, words of *two* syllables, having the accent on the *last* syllable, and terminated by a *single consonant*, preceded by a single vowel, require a duplication of the final consonant when another syllable, beginning with a vowel, is added, as *remit*, *remitting*, &c.

But if the accent be on the *first* syllable, or be removed from the *last* to the first on the addition of another syllable, or if a *diphthong* precede the *final consonant*, no duplication takes place, as *audit*, *auditor*; *refer*, *reference*; *careen*, *careening*.

---

* Vide p. 10.

5. Words ending with any double letter except *l* taking *ness* and *ful* after them, preserve the double consonant, as *careless, carelessness*.

6. *Ness, less, ly, ful*, and *ment*, added to words ending in silent *e*, seldom require the *e* to be elided, as *cease, ceaseless; advertise, advertisement*.

There are a few exceptions to this rule; as *duly, truly, awful, judgment, abridgment, acknowledgment*.

7. *Ing** and *ish*, *able* and *ible* require the elision of the primitive's final *e*, as *lodge, lodging; prude, prudish; cure, curable; sense, sensible*; except *move, moveable*. But if *c* or *g* precede the *e*, it is not elided on the addition of *able*, as *peace, peaceable; change, changeable*. The *e* is here retained to preserve the soft sound of *c* and *g*.

EXERCISES

Containing instances of improper spelling, to be corrected in writing by the pupil.

A careles ladd.
Mufs are made of fur.
One, three five, &c. are od numbers.
The brewer hass taken a but of beer to the road-side in.
A canall is an artificial river.
Unroll the mapp.
Druggs are used in medicines.
The sea ebs.
Pus purs.
The eg is badd.
Flys buz.
To er is human.
The trees budd.
Beetles humm.
Bread is the staf of life.
The finn of a fish.
Youth should not be too fancyfull.
Matts are made of rushes, of hemp, and of wooll.
We are taught to pray for our dayly bread.
The sallys of witt often give offence.
The lowly vallies produce fragrant lilys.
He prefered my cousin's referrence to that of my uncle.
Willfull mistakes are truly awefull.
Christianity sets before us the most blisfull prospects.
By defering repentance we accumulate sorrow.

* "The *e* is sometimes preserved," says Mr. Grant, "for the sake of distinction," on adding *ing*, and adduces *singe* as an example, whose active participle he writes *singeing*, to distinguish it from *singing*, the active participle of *sing*. There does not, however, appear the slightest necessity for departing from the general rule, as the sense will readily direct the pronunciation.

The committee were begining to have the accounts auditted when the meetting broke up.

Laws, both human and divine, are servicable; but the divine laws are not reverseible by the enactments of men.

Let the pupil affix the augments *ing* and *ed* to the following words:—

Satisfy, amuse, annul, annoy, rely, deface, change, rejoice, delay, amaze.

Let him affix *able, ible, ish, ful, ment, ly*, and *ness* to the subjoined, as the sense requires:—

Able, acknowledge, allege, allow, ample, appellative, beauty, body, full, (with *ly* and *ness*,) commence, cure, deduce, duty, drone, elope, judge, force, godly, grace, knave, joy, pity, white, awe, woe.

The following sentences contain errors of frequent occurrence:—

He will seperate the sheep from the goats.

A dilligent observance of men and things will greatly augment our inteligence.

The study of grammer is indispensible to a youth of education.

Though the business alotted to us may be disagreable, we must not shrink from it.

A gaol is the terminus of a race-course; a goal is for the punishment of criminals.

To practice virtue we must exercise self-denial.

Many things are plausable in theory, which fail in practise.

I know a bank were the wild time grows.

Many persons are affraid were their is nothing to afright them.

Camomile is an odoriferous plant.

The pearling brook and the chrystal stream.

The fruit, &c. after dinner are called the desert.

ETYMOLOGY.

ETYMOLOGY teaches the classification of words, their properties, inflections, and derivations.

The English language may be divided into eight* classes, or parts of speech, viz.:

NOUN, PRONOUN, ADNOUN, or ADJECTIVE, VERB, ADVERB, PREPOSITION, CONJUNCTION, and INTERJECTION.

NOUNS.†

A NOUN is the name of any thing that is seen, or that can be imagined.‡

Nouns are either *Proper* or *Common*.

PROPER NOUNS are the names appropriated to the individuals of a species; as *George, England, Humber*. They should always begin with a capital letter.

COMMON, or APPELLATIVE NOUNS, are the names applied to whole species, as *boy, tree, house, town*.

---

* Some writers make ten, or even *twelve* parts of speech; which, instead of elucidating the science of Grammar, tend rather to obscure it. If the language can, without the slightest difficulty, be reduced to *eight* general classes, it seems preposterous to augment that number to *twelve*. The obvious tendency of such increase, is to introduce confusion and complexity into a subject which should be rendered as simple and uncumbered as possible. Of such it may be inquired, "Who is this that darkeneth counsel by words without knowledge?"—Job. xxxviii. 2.

† Sometimes called *Substantives*.

‡ As soon as the pupil has commenced the Noun, the master should teach him to distinguish it from the other parts of speech, by reading to him from some easy book, and requiring him to tell the Nouns in each sentence; and as he learns the Gender, Number, and Person, he should be made to distinguish them accordingly; and so of the other parts of speech as he advances. Such exercises in Etymological parsing, will remove the tedious dryness frequently experienced in the study of Grammar, and will greatly facilitate Syntactical parsing.

Common Nouns may be subdivided into six classes,

1. *Abstract*—as *morality, fortitude, virtue, whiteness,* &c.
2. *Artificial*—as *house, table, desk,* &c.
3. *Collective*—as *nation, multitude, parliament, army,* &c.
4. *Compound*—as *mouse-trap, goat-herd, salt-cellar,* &c.
5. *Natural*—as *river, mountain, valley,* &c.
6. *Verbal*—as *seeing, hearing, dancing, beginning, ending,* &c.

Nouns are subject to *Gender, Number, Person,* and *Case.*

GENDER.

Gender is the distinction of nouns with respect to their sex. Naturally speaking, nouns have but *two* genders, the masculine and feminine; but grammatically speaking they have four, the *masculine, feminine, common,* and *neuter.*

The *masculine* denotes the *males;* the *feminine* the *females;* the *common* those which are either *male* or *female;* and the *neuter* those which are *neither, i. e.* inanimate objects.

In the English language the sexes are thus distinguished.

1. By different words, as—

Male.	*Female.*	*Male.*	*Female.*
Bachelor	Maid, Virgin, Spinster	Drake	Duck
		Earl	Countess
		Father	Mother
Beau	Belle	Friar, Monk	Nun
Boar	Sow	Gaffer	Gammer
Boy	Girl	Gander	Goose
Brother	Sister	Hart	Roe
Buck	Doe	Horse	Mare
Bull	Cow	Husband	Wife
Bullock, or Steer	Heifer	King	Queen
Cock	Hen	Lad	Lass
Colt	Filly	Lord	Lady
Dog	Bitch	Man	Woman

Male.	*Female.*	*Male.*	*Female.*
Master	Mistress / Dame	Sir	Madam
		Sloven	Slut
Milter	Spawner	Son	Daughter
Nephew	Niece	Stag	Hind
Ram / Wether	Ewe	Uncle	Aunt
		Wizard	Witch

2. By a difference of termination, as—

Abbot	Abbess	Hero	Heroine
Actor	Actress	Landgrave	Landgravine
Administrator	Administratrix		
Bridegroom	Bride	Sultan	Sultaness / Sultana
Marquis	Marchioness		
Executor	Executrix	Widower	Widow, &c.

3. By a prefix to the noun.

Male.	*Female.*
A cock-sparrow	A hen-sparrow
A man-servant	A maid-servant
A he-goat	A she-goat
A he-bear	A she-bear
A male-child	A female-child
Male-descendants	Female-descendants

NUMBER.

Nouns are of the *singular* or *plural* number.

The singular implies but *one* object, as *a book, a hat.*

The plural denotes *more* than *one*, as *books, hats.*

The plural of nouns is generally formed by affixing *s* to the singular, as *girl, girls; road, roads; pen, pens.*

The ancient method of forming the plural of nouns was by adding *en* to the singular; a few instances of which still remain, as *ox, oxen; chick, chicken; child, children.* This was the Saxon formation of the plural.*

---

* *Kine* and *swine*, the plural of *cow* and *sow*, have been diverted from the ancient Saxon plural in *en*. *Cowen* has easily been corrupted into *kine*, and *sowen* into *swine*.

By reference to old authors, we find that verbs also took the plural form of *en*; *e. g. hadden* was the plural of *hadde* (had); *weren* of *was*;

Nouns ending in *x*, *ch* (soft), *sh*, *ss*, or *s*, require *es* to be affixed for the plural, as *tax*, *taxes*; *crutch*, *crutches*; *sash*, *sashes*; *moss*, *mosses*; *isthmus*, *isthmuses*.

Some nouns, ending in *o*, require *es*, as *potato*, *potatoes*; but when *i* precedes the *o*, *s* only is added, as *punctilio*, *punctilios*; *folio*, *folios*.

The following nouns ending in *o* have *s* only in the plural, *canto*, *grotto*, *junto*, *portico*, *quarto*, *solo*, *tyro*.

Nouns ending in *ch* (hard), take *s* only in the plural, as *monarch*, *monarchs*; *stomach*, *stomachs*.

Nouns ending in *y*, preceded by a consonant, change the *y* into *i*, and require *es* in addition, as *fly*, *flies*; *beauty*, *beauties*.

This change is adopted because the *y* is now used instead of *ie*, which was the ancient method of spelling such words. In old authors we find *flie*, not *fly*; *beautie*, not *beauty*.

When the *y* is preceded by a vowel, it remains unchanged, and *s* only is added, as *day*, *days*; *boy*, *boys*.*

Some nouns, ending in *f* or *fe*, change the *f* or *fe* into *ves*, in forming the plural, as *sheaf*, *sheaves*; *knife*, *knives*. Of this description there are *fourteen*; while *twenty-seven* nouns of these terminations take *s* only in the plural, as *dwarf*, *gulf*, *roof*, *strife*, &c.

Nouns ending in *ff* take *s*, as *muff*, *muffs*; *ruff*, *ruffs*; except *staff*, which makes *staves*.

Some nouns are the same in both numbers, as *deer*, *sheep*.

Some have no plural, as *gold*, *wheat*, *tea*, &c.

Some of these collective nouns, however, admit a plural, when different sorts of the same commodity are implied, as *teas*, *wines*, *wheats*.

Many nouns form their plurals very irregularly, as

Sing.	*Plural*	*Sing.*	*Plural*	*Sing.*	*Plural*
Man	Men	Foot	Feet	Goose	Geese
Woman	Women	Ox	Oxen	Mouse	Mice
Child	Children	Tooth	Teeth	Louse	Lice

---

schulen of *schal* (shall). "Bothe *weren* juste before God .... And thei *hadden* no child....So thou schult be doumbe til the day in which these thingis *schulen* be don."—*Version of the Gospels, probably written between the time of Alfred and that of the Norman conquest.*

* Some writers change *ey* into *ies* in the plural, and make *chimnies* the pl. of *chimney*; *attornies* the pl. of *attorney*, &c. As this is a needless infraction of an established rule, it is a very reprehensible practice, and ought to be discountenanced.

Die, for throwing chances, makes *dice*; for coining, &c., it makes *dies*: and *index*, in reference to algebraic quantities, becomes *indices* in the plural; but when it refers to tables of contents, *indexes*.

The list of irregular plurals might be much augmented by the introduction of foreign words, which are occasionally adopted. A few of the principal are here subjoined.

Sing.	*Plural*	*Sing.*	*Plural*
Antithesis	Antitheses	Genius	Genii *
Arcanum	Arcana	Memorandum	Memoranda / Memorandums
Automatum	Automata	Metamorphosis	Metamorphoses
Axis	Axes	Monsieur	Messieurs
Basis	Bases	Phenomenon	Phenomena
Beau	Beaux	Radius	Radii
Cherub	Cherubim / Cherubs	Seraph	Seraphim / Seraphs
Crisis	Crises	Stamen	Stamina
Criterion	Criteria	Stimulus	Stimuli
Datum	Data	Vertex	Vertices
Ellipsis	Ellipses	Virtuoso	Virtuosi
Emphasis	Emphases	Vortex	Vortices
Erratum	Errata		
Focus	Foci		

Singular nouns, including many individuals, are called *nouns of multitude*, or *collective nouns*, as *assembly*, *senate*, *people*.

PERSON.

In grammatical language there are three persons, the *first*, *second*, and *third*. The *first person* speaks, the *second* is spoken to, and the *third* is spoken of.

Nouns are of the *third* person, except when addressed, they are then of the *second*.

---

* *Genii*, when denoting aërial spirits; but when indicating persons of superior mental endowments, the *plural* is *geniuses*.

CASE.

Nouns are of the *nominative*, *possessive*, or *objective* case.

In English, the *nominative* and *objective* cases of *nouns* are subject to no variation.

The possessive, which is, in reality, the *only* case that the English noun retains,* is formed by *s* with an apostrophe (*'s*), as *the boy's cap*, *the girl's books*, *the men's work*.

When the noun ends in *s*, the apostrophe is used without appending the *s*, as *for righteousness' sake*, *the boys' school*, *the ladies' seminary*.

The names of persons, and some words ending in *s*, frequently require the apostrophic *s*, as *Jones's library*, *Bliss's books*, *the ass's ears*, &c.

In some instances, also, even where the noun does not terminate in *s*, the apostrophe only is used, and the *s* is omitted, as *for conscience' sake*, *for elegance' sake*. Here the additional *s* would occasion a hissing sound, and much difficulty of pronunciation.

The Saxon ending of this case, as also of the plural number,† was *is* or *es*, as "*knitis*" for *knight's*. CHAUCER; "*leavis*" for *leaves*. SPENCER. This was in general use till about the middle of the 16th century, when the vowel was superseded by the apostrophe.

An example of this *genitive* form is still retained in the Book of Common Prayer. The "Prayer for all Conditions of Men" closes thus, "*for Christis sake*," which, through ignorance of its original formation, is now generally printed, "*for Christ his sake*."

This case marks the *possessor*, or that to which something belongs, as *the queen's crown*, *the governor's house*.

---

* It is only by accommodation that any but the possessive case can be applied to the English language. Case is a terminational change or *falling*, as the word implies, *i. e.* from the nominative singular. The noun in its *first form* was called *upright* (rectus); the variations from that form were called *cases*.

† "He schal turne the *hertis* of the *fadris* to the *sonis*."—*Version of the Gospels before the Conquest*.

Sometimes the latter noun is omitted, as *I am going to St. Paul's. I dined yesterday at my cousin's.*

The *nominative* and *objective* cases of nouns can only be properly communicated in *parsing*, which should be sedulously pursued as soon as the pupil is acquainted with the *Verb*. This will greatly facilitate the acquisition of grammatical knowledge.

EXERCISES.

The lions (*pl.*) den.
The poem consists of eight cantoes.
Flys are troublesome in summer.
I am going to dine at my brothers.
The fashion is adopted for elegance sake.
Have you seen St. Pauls Cathedral?
Potatos are not indiginous to England.
There were many erratums in the book.
The Arabian nights tales.
The attorneys clerk is at my fathers.
Attornies abound in England
I have seen the Queen's of England's carriage.

Spell the plural of the following nouns—

Lass, army, brush, table, city, delay, dandy, fox, grandee, hero, inch, jelly, knife, roof, stomach, negro, penny, prospectus, distich, cargo, hoof, solo, stamen, scarf, stratum, watch, whiff, die, dwarf, fife, life, fish, folio, genius, grotto, handkerchief, radius, seraph, tooth, sheep, cherub, ox.

Correct the errors in the following sentences—

How long has Charles been a widow?
Have you heard that Mary has become a bridegroom?
Your sister has become quite a giant in statute.
In Scott's Kenilworth, Amy Robsart is the hero of the tale.
Mr. B. has left his wife sole executor. In her own will she will be testator.
The stature of William IV., and that of the Duke of Wellington's, are ornamental to the city.
In point of statute they are both colossal.
The statues in the English code have lately received many alterations.

PRONOUNS.

Pronouns supply the place of nouns, and thus obviate the necessity of their repetition. They are relative words, and correspond with some antecedent or correlative.*

The chief pronouns are—*I*, *thou*, *he*, *she*, *it*; with their plurals *we*, *ye or you*, *they*: and *who*, *which*, *that*, and *what* of both numbers.

They are of the *masculine*, *feminine*, *common*, or *neuter* gender.

They are of the *singular* or *plural* number.

They are of the *first*, *second*, or *third* person.

They are of the *nominative*, *possessive*, or *objective* case.

The *gender*, *number*, *person*, and *case* of *I*, *thou*, *he*, *she*, *it*, will be easily acquired by becoming familiar with their declension.

First Person, Common Gender.

Sing.		*Plural*	
Nom.	I	*Nom.*	We
Poss.	Mine	*Poss.*	Ours
Ob.	Me	*Ob.*	Us

Second Person, Common Gender.

Nom.	Thou	*Nom.*	Ye or you
Poss.	Thine	*Poss.*	Yours
Ob.	Thee	*Ob.*	You

Third Person, Masculine Gender.

Sing.		*Plural*	
Nom.	He	*Nom.*	They
Poss.	His	*Poss.*	Theirs
Ob.	Him	*Ob.*	Them

Third Person, Feminine Gender.

Nom.	She	*Nom.*	They
Poss.	Hers	*Poss.*	Theirs
Ob.	Her	*Ob.*	Them

Third Person, Neuter Gender.

Sing.		*Plural*	
Nom.	It	*Nom.*	They
Poss.	Its	*Poss.*	Theirs
Ob.	It	*Ob.*	Them

The gender of pronouns except that of *he*, *she*, *it*, can only be ascertained by the nouns which they represent.

Myself, *thyself*, *himself*, *&c.*, properly come under the description of *pronouns*; they are of a compound quality, and may be termed *reflective pronouns*.

Pronouns are of the same *gender*, *number*, and *person*, as the words to which they relate.

* The term *correlative* is preferable to *antecedent*, because the word or clause which the pronoun represents is not unfrequently *subsequent* to that pronoun, it cannot then be an *antecedent*.

Who and *which*, of both numbers, are thus declined :—

Sing. & Plural		*Sing. & Plural*	
Nom.	Who	*Nom.*	Which
Poss.	Whose	*Poss.*	Whose
Ob.	Whom	*Ob.*	Which

Who is always applied to persons, *which* to irrational animals and things inanimate, as "the girl *who* plays," "the cow *which* is milked," "the tree *which* is barren."

When inanimate objects are personified, *who* is frequently used instead of *which*, as in the following couplet :—

> "Fair Liberty, *who* now in Britain rears
> *Her* cheerful head, and leads the golden years."

That is sometimes used to obviate the tautology of *who* and *which.*

What is sometimes a pronoun, including in itself both the *relative* and the *antecedent*, and is tantamount to *that which*, or the *thing which*, as "Father, forgive them, for they know not *what* they do," *i. e.* the thing which, &c.

What, when joined to a *noun*, becomes an *adnoun* ; as "*What evil hath he done?*"

Whoso, *whosoever*, *whoever*, *whether*, are also pronouns ; they are however seldom used by modern writers, as—

"WHOSOEVER *will, let him take the water of life freely ;*"
"WHETHER *of the twain did the will of his father?*"

ADNOUNS,* OR ADJECTIVES.

Adnouns belong to *nouns*, and can *never* be used without them.

They may be divided into five classes, viz., the *qualifying*, the *pronominal*, the *demonstrative*, the *numeral*, and the *indefinite*.

QUALIFYING ADNOUNS express some quality of the nouns to which they belong, as *an obedient son, an affectionate daughter*.

---

* The term *adnoun* is used in preference to *adjective*, as conveying a more definite idea of the nature of this part of speech, *joined to a noun*.

Qualifying Adnouns in English are not susceptible of either concord or regimen.*

The only variation to which they are subject is that of *comparison.*

Of this, there are, *accurately speaking,* but *two degrees,*† the comparative and the superlative.

The *positive,* which is *erroneously* called a degree, is the simple state‡ of the adnoun, as *plain, fine.*

The comparative degree of *monosyllabic* adnouns is generally formed by affixing *r* or *er* to the *positive state;* and the *superlative* by affixing *st* or *est,* as—

Positive	*Comparative*	*Superlative*
Fine	Finer	Finest
Plain	Plainer	Plainest

Polysyllabic adnouns, with few exceptions, are compared by prefixing *more* and *most,* or *less* and *least,* as—

Positive	*Comparative*	*Superlative*
Favourable	More favourable	Most favourable
Beautiful	More beautiful	Most beautiful
Expensive	Less expensive	Least expensive

Monosyllables ending in double *e,* are more appropriately compared by *more* and *most,* as—

Positive	*Comparative*	*Superlative*
Free	More free	Most free

Sometimes, when *emphasis* is required, adjectives of one syllable are advantageously compared by *more* and *most.*

When the positive state of a monosyllabic adnoun ends in a single consonant, preceded by a single vowel, the consonant is doubled in forming the degrees of comparison, as—

Positive	*Comparative*	*Superlative*
Fit	Fitter	Fittest
Big	Bigger	Biggest§

* In this respect the English differs from most languages, ancient and modern.

† It is evident that, in nature, gradations must be innumerable. How many degrees subsist between a *mouse* and an *elephant*—a *molehill* and a *mountain!* Still in grammar there are only two degrees.

‡ A degree implies a step either higher or lower, which is not the case with the positive state.

§ Vide Orthography, Rule 4, p. 4.

The subjoined are irregularly compared:—

Positive	*Comparative*	*Superlative*
Good	Better	Best
Bad	Worse	Worst
Little	Less	Least
Much, or many	More	Most
Late	Later, or latter	Latest, or last
Near	Nearer	Nearest, or next
Far	Farther	Farthest
Fore	Former	Foremost, or first
Old	Older, or elder	Oldest, or eldest
	Upper	Uppermost
	Under	Undermost
	Exterior	Extreme
	Superior	Supreme

PRONOMINAL ADNOUNS are derived from the possessive case of the pronouns, *I*, *thou*, *he*, *she*, *it*, *we*, *you*, *they*,—and denote property or possession; they are *my*, *thy*, *his*, *her*, *its*, *our*, *your*, *their*, and *own*, which is always used with one of the foregoing to mark particular stress, as *my book*, *his hat*, *our own country*.

Mine and *thine* are used in the Holy Scriptures before a vowel, as "I kept myself from *mine* iniquity."—Ps. xviii. 23. "Let *thine* eyes be open, and let *thine* ears be attent."—2 Chron. vi. 40.

DEMONSTRATIVE ADNOUNS emphatically point out the *nouns* with which they are connected:—they are *this* and *that*, with their plurals *these and those;* and *the*, which is not affected by number.

This refers to an object near the speaker,—*that* to one more distant. *This* points to the *latter* of two circumstances mentioned in a sentence,—*that* to the *former*, as "*This* person is more intelligent than *that*." "Religion ennobles mankind; irreligion degrades them:—*that* assimilates them to angels; *this* degenerates them below the brutes."

"My bane and antidote are both before me:
That in a moment brings me to an end;
But *this* informs me I shall never die."—ADDISON.

NUMERAL ADNOUNS are the numbers, and are either—

Cardinal, as 1, 2, 3, &c; or
Ordinal, as 1st, 2nd, 3rd, &c.

INDEFINITE ADNOUNS convey a general and undefined idea of the nouns to which they are joined:—they are such words as, *some*, *other*,* *a* or *an*, *any*, *one*, *all*, *such*, *else*, *both*, *whole*, *no*, *none*, *another*, *each*, *every*, *either*, *neither*; the last four are always connected with nouns in the singular number.

A or *an*, and *the* are generally denominated *articles*; but they are, with strict propriety, classed among the demonstrative and indefinite adnouns:—*the* being *demonstrative*, and *a* or *an indefinite*.

A is used before a word beginning with a consonant; or *u* when it forms a syllable by itself,—also before an aspirated *h*, as *a man*, *a unicorn*, *a house*; *an* is used before words commencing with a *vowel*, a *u*, when it does not form a distinct syllable, and an unaspirated *h*, as *an acorn*, *an umpire*, *an heiress*.

Write the comparative and superlative of—

Sad, thin, coy, silly, faithful, grave, good, large, ill, little, bad, pretty, beautiful, true, sure, strange.

Correct the errors in the following expressions—

An older sister.—The oldest uncle.

He is the tallest of the two.

An industrious scholer is happyer than an idler.

Spring is the elasticest season of the year; sumer is the hotest; autum is the fruitfullest; winter is the gloomyest, but the convivialest.

James is biger than his brother, but not gooder.

The cothage is built at the most extreme edge of the forest.

An union between England and Scotland.

I have a uncle in America.

He was an hero.

PROMISCUOUS EXERCISES.

Man eats a grater variety of food than the bruit creation. He may be entitled a carniverous, a grameniverous, a pisiverous, and a fructiverous animal. He eats the wild game of the forrest,—the partridge, the hair, the phesant, and the dear. The ox affords him beefe; the sheap, mutton; and the pig and the calf furnish his table with pork and veel.

---

* Other takes a plural; but then it ceases to be an *adnoun*.

The crops of the field wave for him—and yield him wheet for his bread—barly for his ail,—and a variety of other grain for domestic purposes.

The garden affords him esculent herbs and edible roots,—the meely potatoe, the delicate cawleflower, the homely cabage, the sparagras, the coucumber, the carat, the turnep, and the bulbous onyan. He makes a coolling salade of the lettice, the raddish, the endive, and the salery, with the warm mustard and cress.

The well-stocked garden also produces for his gratification the jucy apple, and the deliscious pare, the pulpey chery, the blooming plumb, the peech, and the rosey apricock and nectarine. He there gathers the strawbury, the current, the goosbury, and the fragrant raspbury.

He levies supplies for his apetite from the briney deep and the meandering river—whence is table is occasionaly furnished with the carp, the sallmon, and the trout,—the codd, the turbert, and the hering,—the crabb, the lobster, the oister, and the eele.

Well might David say—"Thou madest him to have dominion over the works of thy hands; thou hast put all things under is feat; all sheap and oxen; yea, and the beastes of the field, the foul of the hare, and the fish of the see,—and whatsoever passeth through the paths of the sees."

VERB.

The Verb* is the principal part of speech in every language, and it is susceptible of considerable variation both as to form and meaning.

Verbs are words that generally denote action, and as such are either transitive† or intransitive, as *I strike, he walks.*

Some also assert existence, or a state of being;

---

* From *verbum* (word), which is characteristic of its importance. It is *the word* (verbum) by way of eminence.

† *Transitive* from *transeo, I pass over. Intransitive* is obviously formed by a negative prefix.

and as such may be termed *quiescent verbs*, as *I am, thou sittest, he sleeps.**

Every verb requires a *subject* or *agent* which is the nominative case to the verb; and this is either a *noun* or a *pronoun.*

Transitive verbs are words in which the action passes from the *agent* to an *object*, as "John beats the horse;" where the action passes from *John*, as the *agent*, to the *horse*, as the *object.*

The *object* of a transitive verb is either a *noun* or *pronoun.*

Transitive verbs have two voices, active and passive.†

John kicks the horse, is *active:*—John is kicked by the horse, is *passive.*

In the *former*, the *agent* is the nominative case; in the *latter*, the *object* is the nominative.

Intransitive verbs are words in which the action *does not pass* from the *agent* to an *object*, as *John runs, Charles walks, the boys play, the cock crows.*

Verbs are subject to the inflection of *mood, tense, number,* and *person,*—and these are called the *accidents* of the verb.

There are four moods, viz.—

The *Indicative*, which indicates or affirms, as "God created the world."

---

* The usual division of verbs into active, passive, and neuter, is contrary to common sense. It is quite inconsistent to talk of neuter verbs in opposition to active and passive. The word *neuter* signifies *neither;* it therefore implies that such verbs express neither *action* nor *passion*, which is opposed to fact; for what grammarians term *neuter* verbs do express action, *e. g. I run, he walks*, &c. Much more objectionable is the division of verbs into *active* and *inactive*, by which such verbs as *dance, skip, fly, swim, climb*, &c. are doomed to a state of inaction!

† Some grammarians have attempted to expunge the passive voice from the English Grammar; but their reasons are not sufficiently cogent to authorise the adoption of such a course. It is very true that we are compelled to employ an auxiliary with the passive participle of the verb throughout its conjugation. And is not the Latin verb obliged to adopt a similar method in the formation of several of its tenses in the passive voice? To make the participle a separate division of speech, seems an unnecessary incumbrance to the machinery of grammatical science; and to call it a *verbal adnoun* is equally objectionable. The import of an *adnoun* and a participle is very different:—"*The man is criminal,*" denotes a certain quality of the man; *criminal* is therefore an *adnoun*. *The man is imprisoned*, expresses some passive endurance to which he is *subjected.* His *criminality* has been voluntary on his part; but his *imprisonment* has been *imposed* upon him *against* his will.

The *Imperative*, which commands or entreats, as "Remember now thy Creator."

The *Potential*, which denotes power or permission; possibility or will, as "Lord if thou wilt, thou *canst make* me clean."

The *Infinitive*, which expresses only the simple state of the verb in an unlimited form, is known by *to* being always expressed or understood before it.* It is not subject to any inflections, like the other moods.

TENSE.

Tense signifies time; of which, naturally speaking, there are but *three* divisions,– the *present*, the *past*, and the *future*; but grammatically speaking, it may be subdivided into *six*† parts, viz., the *present*, the *past*, the *perfect*, the *perfect anterior*, the *future*, and the *future anterior*.‡

The PRESENT is indivisible; it is but the passing moment, as *I write.*

The PAST is susceptible of *three subdivisions*, viz., the *past*, the *perfect*, and the *perfect anterior*. The past expresses the completion of an action in a period of time entirely elapsed, as *I wrote a letter yesterday*:–the *perfect* describes the completion of an action in a period of time, of which *part has yet to elapse*, as *I have written a letter to-day*:—the *perfect*

---

* Some grammarians controvert the existence of such a mood in English.—"It is evidently a verbal noun," says one; but what the evidence is does not appear. It is indeed evident that the English must have an *infinitive mood*; and it has no other means of supplying that necessity than by resorting to the particle "*to*," in composition with the verb. *To err, to forgive*, are as much *infinitives* in *English*, as *errare, ignoscere*, are in *Latin*. *To love, to write, to speak*, claim as much to be *infinitives* in *English*, as *aimer, écrire, parler*, do in *French*.

† The English verb admits of such limited inflection as to produce only *two pure* tenses, the *present* and the *past*: but the exigencies of the language require other tenses, and these can be formed only by combination—hence the employment of auxiliaries; and their assistance imparts such *richness, beauty*, and *expression* to the English tongue, as to give it a superiority over most other languages.

‡ The divisions of Murray are exposed to many objections. His "imperfect" is an anomaly; his "pluperfect" is equally objectionable, as an action cannot be more than *perfect*: perfect *anterior* is more accurate, as implying that the action was complete prior to a certain event or time. And the division of the future tenses into first and second, gives no idea whatever of their meaning. Future and future anterior are more in accordance with the philosophy of grammar.

anterior represents the completion of an action *prior* to a *certain* event, as *I had written my letter before your brother arrived.*

The FUTURE admits of *two subdivisions*, viz., the *future*, and the *future anterior*:—the *future* denotes an action *yet to come*, as *I will write*:—the *future anterior* indicates an action to be completed *before the arrival of a certain event*, as *I shall have written my letter before the departure of your brother.*

Verbs have *two numbers*, the *singular* and the *plural*.

They have *three persons*; the *first*, *second*, and *third*.

They have *two* participles, the *present* or *active*, and the *past* or *passive*, as—

Present or active.	*Past or Passive.*
Accosting *	accosted.

They are either *regular* or *irregular*.

A *regular verb* forms the *past tense* and *passive participle* by the addition of *d*, or *ed* to the verb, as—

Present.	*Past tense.*	*Passive participle.*
Save	saved	saved
Accost	accosted	accosted

An irregular verb deviates from this rule, as—

Present.	*Past tense.*	*Past participle.*
Write	wrote	written
Buy	bought	bought

Every *finite verb* (*i. e.* a verb not in the infinitive mood) must have an *agent*, which is the *nominative*; and every *transitive verb* must have an *object*, which is the *objective case*.

The conjugation † of a verb is the management of all its variations with regard to *mood*, *tense*, *number*, and *person*.

Conjugation of the regular transitive verb—Accost.

Present.	*Past.*	*Past Participle.*
Accost	accosted	accosted

INFINITIVE MOOD.

Pr. To accost. *Perf.* To have accosted.

---

* The *active participle always* ends in *ing*.

† The term signifies *yoking together*, implying that all the parts of the verb are thereby united.

INDICATIVE MOOD.*—*Present tense.*

Sing.	*Plural.*
1. I accost	1. We accost
2. Thou accostest	2. You accost
3. He, she, or it accosts	3. They accost
Or—	
1. I do accost	1. We do accost
2. Thou dost accost	2. You do accost
3. He does accost	3. They do accost

Past.

1. I accosted	1. We accosted
2. Thou accostedst	2. You accosted
3. He accosted	3. They accosted
Or—	
1. I did accost	1. We did accost
2. Thou didst accost	2. You did accost
3. He did accost	3. They did accost

Perfect.

1. I have accosted	1. We have accosted
2. Thou hast accosted	2. You have accosted
3. He has accosted	3. They have accosted

Perfect anterior.

1. I had accosted	1. We had accosted
2. Thou hadst accosted	2. You had accosted
3. He had accosted	3. They had accosted

Future.—(Shall or will.)

1. I shall accost	1. We shall accost
2. Thou shalt accost	2. You shall accost
3. He shall accost	3. They shall accost

Future anterior.—(Shall or will have.)

1. I shall have accosted	1. We shall have accosted
2. Thou shalt have accosted	2. You shall have accosted
3. He shall have accosted	3. They shall have accosted

---

* The terminational variations of the *indicative mood* are often omitted, when condition, contingency, or end is expressed, as "Love not sleep, lest thou *come* to poverty."—Prov. xx. 13. "Except the Lord *keep* the city, the watchman waketh but in vain."—Ps. cxxvii. 1. In most cases of this kind there is an ellipsis in the phraseology.

IMPERATIVE MOOD.

Sing.	*Plural.*
2. { Accost, or Do thou accost	2. { Accost, or* Do you accost

POTENTIAL MOOD.

Present tense.—(May, can, or must.)

1. I may accost	1. We may accost
2. Thou mayst accost	2. You may accost
3. He may accost	3. They may accost

Past.—(Might, could, would, or should.)

1. I might accost	1. We might accost
2. Thou mightst accost	2. You might accost
3. He might accost	3. They might accost

Perfect.—(May, can, or must have.)

1. I may have accosted	1. We may have accosted
2. Thou mayst have accosted	2. You may have accosted
3. He may have accosted	3. They may have accosted

Perfect anterior.—(Might, could, would, or should have.)

1. I might have accosted	1. We might have accosted
2. Thou mightst have accosted	2. You might have accosted
3. He might have accosted	3. They might have accosted

PARTICIPLES.

Active.†	*Passive.*
Accosting	Accosted

The passive voice is formed by affixing the passive participle

---

* As this mood is used to entreat, to command, to deprecate, &c., it is obvious that the *second person* only can be employed. When grammarians attempt to make a *first* or *third* person by the aid of *let*, they place the *conjugated* verb in the *infinitive*, and use *let* in the second person, as *let me advise, let me speak.* It is evident that *let* has here the sense of *allow* or *permit*. Change the verb, and the reasoning will appear conclusive,—*allow me to advise, permit me to speak.*

† The active participle is sometimes used as a noun; but as it is deficient in elegance, it should be avoided, as "The moral law consists in the *obeying* of God and the *loving* of our neighbour." This mode of expression is very cumbersome. "*Obedience* to God, and *love* to our neighbour," is preferable.

of a transitive verb to the verb *to be;* which is thus conjugated: *

Present.	*Past.*	*Passive Participle.*
Am, be	was	been

INFINITIVE MOOD.

Present. To be. *Perfect.* To have been.

INDICATIVE MOOD.—*Present tense.*

Sing.	*Plural.*
1. I am (be †) accosted	1. We are (be) accosted
2. Thou art (be'st) accosted	2. You are (be) accosted
3. He is (be) accosted	3. They are (be) accosted

Past tense.

1. I was (were ‡) accosted	1. We were accosted
2. Thou wast (were) accosted	2. You were accosted
3. He was (were) accosted	3. They were accosted

Perfect tense.—(Have.)

1. I have been accosted	1. We have been accosted
2. Thou hast been accosted	2. You have been accosted
3. He has been accosted	3. They have been accosted

Perfect anterior.—(Had.)

1. I had been accosted	1. We had been accosted
2. Thou hadst been accosted	2. You had been accosted
3. He had been accosted	3. They had been accosted

* The author recommends the verb *be* to be carefully studied, before using it in the passive form; when perfectly acquired, the passive participle may be added, and the passive voice will then be easily attained.

† This verb appears to be very irregular in all languages. Formerly *be* was used in all the persons of the present tense, as we find in the Bible, "Jehu said to all the people, ye *be* righteous."—2 Kings x. 9. "Narrow is the way which leadeth unto life, and few there *be* that find it."—Matt. vii. 14.

Be is *now* always used when doubt, condition, contingency, or end is expressed, as "And Isaac said unto Jacob, come near, that I may feel thee, whether thou *be* my son Esau."—Gen. xxvii. 21. "If God *be* for us, who can be against us?"—Rom. viii. 31.

‡ *Were* and *wert* are used in the singular, where doubt, contingency, &c. are expressed.

Future.—(Shall, will.)

Sing.	*Plural.*
1. I shall be accosted	1. We shall be accosted
2. Thou shalt be accosted	2 You shall be accosted
3. He shall be accosted	3. They shall be accosted

Future anterior.—(Shall, will, have.)

1. I shall have been accosted	1. We shall have been accosted
2. Thou shalt have been accosted	2. You shall have been accosted
3. He shall have been accosted	3. They shall have been accosted

IMPERATIVE MOOD.

2. Be, or be thou accosted	2. Be, or be ye accosted

POTENTIAL MOOD.

Present tense.—(May, can, must.)

1. I may be accosted	1. We may be accosted
2. Thou mayst be accosted	2. You may be accosted
3. He may be accosted	3. They may be accosted

Past.—(Might, could, would, should.)

1. I might be accosted	1. We might be accosted
2. Thou mightst be accosted	2. You might be accosted
3. He might be accosted	3. They might be accosted

Perfect.—(May, can, must, have.)

1. I may have been accosted	1. We may have been accosted
2. Thou mayst have been accosted	2. You may have been accosted
3. He may have been accosted	3. They may have been accosted

Perfect anterior.—(Might, could, would, should have.)

1. I might have been accosted	1. We might have been accosted
2 Thou mightst have been accosted	2. You might have been accosted
3. He might have been accosted	3. They might have been accosted

PARTICIPLES.

Present, or *Active*.	*Passive*.
Being	been

The *active* participle of *any* verb affixed to the verb *be*, affords another mode of active conjugation. This may be called the *progressive* form, as it indicates that the action is in a *continued* state.

Thus, there are *three* forms of active conjugation in the *present* and *past* tenses of the verb; and *two* of *all the remaining tenses*.

Present tense.—Singular.

1*st Form.*	2*nd Form.*	3*rd Form.*
I advise	I do advise	I am advising
Thou advisest	Thou dost advise	Thou art advising
He advises, &c.	He does advise, &c.	He is advising, &c.

Past tense.—Singular.

I advised	I did advise	I was advising
&c.	&c.	&c.

Perfect tense.—Singular.

1*st Form.*	2*nd Form.*
I have advised	I have been advising
&c.	&c.

And so on through the subsequent parts of the verb.

Some verbs are called "*Impersonal;*" the title however is not strictly proper, as they are used in the *third* person; they may, with greater propriety, be termed *third personal verbs*, as *it rains*, *it snows*, &c.

The neuter pronoun *it* is frequently used in this arbitrary sense, without reference to any expressed or supposed *correlative;* it is also used in connexion with a noun or pronoun of the *masculine* or *feminine* gender—"Jesus said, *It is I:*" "*It was a lady* who called." This is an anomaly; but it is established in the language.

The same expression is sometimes used in plural construction; thus, *It is they* who are the real authors; *it was* the *heretics* who raised the persecution. In these and similar instances, the mode of composition may be advantageously altered, and the anomaly superseded, thus,—*They* are the real, &c. The heretics raised, &c.

The following is a list of the Irregular Verbs in the English language:—

Present.	Past.	Past. Part.	Present.	Past.	Past Part.
Abide	abode	abode	Clothe	clothed or clad	clad
Am (from *be*)	was	been	Come, *be-*	came	come
Arise	arose	arisen	Cost	cost	cost
Awake	awoke R*	awaked	Crow	crew R	crowed
Bear, *to bring forth.*	bore † bare	born	Creep	crept	crept
			Cut	cut	cut
Bear, *to carry*	bore, bare	borne	Dare, *to venture*	durst	dared
			Dare, *to*	*challenge,*	*is regular*
Beat	beat	beaten, or beat	Deal	dealt R	dealt R
			Dig	dug R	dug R
Begin	began	begun	Do, *mis- un-* §	did	done
Bend	bent R	bent R			
Bereave	bereft R	bereft R	Draw, *with-*	drew	drawn
Beseech	besought	besought			
Bid, *for-*	bad, bade	bidden	Drink	drank	drunk
Bind, *un-*	bound	bound	Drive	drove	driven
Bite	bit	bitten, bit	Dwell	dwelt R	dwelt R
Bleed	bled	bled	Eat	ate *or* eat	eaten
Blow	blew	blown	Fall, *be-*	fell	fallen
Break	broke	broken	Feed	fed	fed
Breed	bred	bred	Feel	felt	felt
Bring	brought	brought	Fight	fought	fought
Build, *re-*	built ‡	built	Find	found	found
Burst	burst	burst	Flee	fled	fled
Buy	bought	bought	Fling	flung	flung
Cast	cast	cast	Fly	flew	flown
Catch	caught	caught	Forbear	forbore	forborn
Chide	chid	chidden or chid	Forsake	forsook	forsaken
			Freeze	froze	frozen
Choose	chose	chosen	Get, *be- for-*	got ‖	got, gotten**
Cleave, *to adhere*	clave R	cleaved	Gild	gilt R	gilt R
Cleave, *to split*	clove, clave or cleft	cloven or cleft	Gird *be- en-*	girt R	girt R
			Give, *for- mis-*	gave	given
Cling	clung	clung			

* Those verbs which are conjugated regularly, as well as irregularly, are marked with an R.

† Bore is now more used than *bare*.

‡ *Build, dwell,* and several other verbs, have the regular form, *builded, dwelled,* &c.

§ The compound verbs are conjugated like the simple, by prefixing the syllables appended to them thus, *undo, undid, undone.*

‖ *Gat* and *begat* are often used in the Scriptures for *got* and *begot.*

** *Gotten* is nearly *obsolete.* Its compound, *forgotten,* is still in good use.

Present.	Past.	Past Part.
Go	went *	gone
Grave, *en-* R	graved	graven
Grind	ground	ground
Grow	grew	grown
Hang	hung	hung †
Have	had	had
Hear	heard	heard
Heave	hove R	heaved
Hew, *rough*	hewed	hewn R
Hide	hid	hidden, *or* hid
Hit	hit	hit
Hold, *be-* *with-*	held	held holden ‡
Hurt	hurt	hurt
Keep	kept	kept
Knit	knit R	knit R
Know	knew	known
Lade	laded	laden
Lay, *in-*	laid	laid
Lead, *mis-*	led	led
Leave	left	left
Lend	lent	lent
Let	let	let
Lie, *lie down*	lay	lain, *or* lien
Load	loaded	laden R
Lose	lost	lost
Make	made	made
Mean	meant	meant
Meet	met	met
Mow	mowed	mown R
Pay, *re-*	paid	paid
Pût	pût	pût
Read	read	read
Rend	rent	rent
Rid	rid	rid
Ride	rode	ridden, *or* rode
Ring	rang *or* rung	rung
Rise, *a-*	rose	risen
Rive	rived	riven
Run	ran	run
Saw	sawed	sawn R
Say	said	said
See	saw	seen
Seek	sought	sought
Seethe	sod R	sodden
Sell	sold	sold
Send	sent	sent
Set, *be-*	set	set
Shake	shook	shaken
Shape, *mis-*	shaped	shapen R
Shave	shaved	shaven
Shear	shore R	shorn
Shed	shed	shed
Shine	shone R	shone R
Shoe	shod	shod
Shoot	shot	shot
Show §	showed	shown
Shrink	shrunk, *or* shrank	shrunk
Shred	shred	shred
Shut	shut	shut
Sing	sang, *or* sung	sung
Sink	sank, *or* sunk	sunk
Sit	sat	sat, *or* sitten
Slay	slew	slain
Sleep	slept	slept
Slide	slid	slidden
Sling	slang, *or* slung	slung
Slink	slank, *or* slunk	slunk
Slit	slit R	slit R
Smite	smote	smitten
Sow	sowed	sown R
Speak, *be-*	spoke, *or* spake	spoken
Speed	sped	sped
Spend, *mis-*	spent	spent
Spill	spilt R	spilt R

* *Go* has no past tense; its place is supplied from the old verb *wend*, now nearly obsolete.

† *Hang*, to take away life by hanging, is regular, as the robber was *hanged*; but the gown was *hung* up.

‡ *Holden* is chiefly used in legal instruments and public notices, thus, "A vestry will be holden."

§ Or *shew*, *shewed*, *shewn*,—pronounced show, &c.

Present.	Past.	Past Part.
Spin	span, *or* spun	spun
Spit	spit, *or* spat	spit, *or* spitten
Split	split	split
Spread, *be-*	spread	spread
Spring	sprang, *or* sprung	sprung
Stand, *with, &c*	stood	stood
Steal	stole	stolen
Stick	stuck	stuck
Sting	stung, *or* stang	stung
Stink	stunk, *or* stank	stunk
Stride, *be-*	strode, *or* strid	stridden, *or* strode
Strike	struck	struck, *or* stricken
String	strung, *or* strang	strung
Strive	strove	striven
Strew,* *be-*	strewed	strewed, *or*
Strow	strowed	strown R
Swear	swore, *or* sware	sworn
Sweat	sweat R	sweat R
Sweep	swept	swept
Swell	swelled	swollen R
Swim	swam, *or* swum	swum
Swing	swang, *or* swung	swung
Take, *be-* *&c.*	took	taken
Teach, *mis- re-*	taught	taught
Tear, *un-*	tore	torn
Tell	told	told
Think	thought	thought
Thrive	throve	thriven
Throw	threw	thrown
Thrust	thrust	thrust
Tread	trod	trodden
Wax	waxed	waxen R
Wear	wore	worn
Weave	wove	woven
Weep	wept	wept
Win	won	won
Wind	wound	wound
Work	wrought R	wrought
Wring	wrung	wrung
Write	wrote	written

Defective verbs are those which want some of their moods and tenses :—

Present.	Past
Can	could
May	might
Must	must
Ought	ought
	quoth
Shall	should
Will	would
Wis	wist
Wit, *or* Wot	wot

ADVERB.

Adverbs belong to *Verbs*, to *Adnouns*, and to other *Adverbs*.

When they belong to *verbs*, they point out the *time*, *place*, or *manner* of the action, as, I rise *early*; *whence* camest thou? he reads *correctly*.

* *Strew* and *shew* are now giving way to *strow* and *show*, as they are pronounced.

When they belong to *adnouns*, or other *adverbs*, they are used to qualify them, as, a *truly* good man; he conducts himself very *discreetly*.

Adverbs ending in *ly*, and a few others, may be compared, as *prudently, more prudently, most prudently; often, oftener, oftenest; soon, sooner, soonest; well, better, best.*

Adverbs ending in *ly* are mostly derived from adnouns, thus,

Quiet	quietly	Rough	roughly
Sober	soberly	Quick	quickly

Yesterday, to-day, to-morrow. "These words," says Lennie, "are always nouns." Doubtless, in some situations they are *nouns*; but in their general use they are *adverbs*, as much as *formerly, immediately, forthwith, hereafter.* In the following instances, they are used *nominally*:—"*To-day's* lesson was more instructive than *yesterday's*; and *to-morrow's* will be still more so." "A thousand years in thy sight, are but as *yesterday* when it is past"—Ps. xc. 14. "Beside all this, *to-day* is the third day."—Luke xxiv. 21. "*To-morrow* shall be as this day, and much more abundant."—Isa. lvi. 12.

Commonly speaking, however, they are adverbs, as "Yesterday at the seventh hour the fever left him."—John iv. 52. "To-day shalt thou be with me in paradise."—Luke xxiii. 42. "To-morrow, said he, thou shalt hear him."—Acts xxv. 22.

PREPOSITION.

Prepositions are principally connected with *Nouns* and *Pronouns*, and govern them in the Objective case, as—The journey *from* London *to* York was performed *by* him.

The following may be considered as the chief Prepositions:—

MONOSYLLABLES.—*At, by, for, from, in, of, on, through, to, with.*

DISSYLLABLES.—*Above, about, after, against, among* or *amongst, before, behind, below, beneath, beside, between* or *betwixt, beyond, into, over, towards, under, unto, within, without.*

To prefixed to a verb, places it in the Infinitive Mood. In that situation it can scarcely be called a preposition,—it is an auxiliary particle.

CONJUNCTION.

Conjunctions serve to unite *words*, *phrases*, and *simple sentences;* as, *three* and *two are five. Foreign idioms* and *unauthorised expressions are improper*,—"*Chasten thy son* while *there is hope.*"

The following is a list of the principal Conjunctions. Some of these may also be *adverbs*, and some *prepositions*, &c.; but that depends upon their signification in a sentence, and can easily be determined by an ordinary grammarian.

*And, as, because, both, but, either, else, except, for, how, if, lest, neither, nor, notwithstanding, or, since, so, than, that, then, therefore, though, unless, wherefore.**

INTERJECTION.

Interjections are used in apostrophising, or in making an exclamation, as, *O ye hypocrites! Ah, me! what mischief have I done.*

DERIVATION.

Having noticed the classification of words, their properties and inflections, the only subject which now remains under Etymology, is *Derivation*, which treats of the *origin* of words, and traces them to their primary *import*.

Many words, though apparently unconnected, will be found to have an identity of origin, when traced to their source.

Thus the words *fable*, *fate* (which literally signifies *spoken*), *fatal, fatalist, affable, ineffable, fabulous, confabulation, fame, infamy, defame, defamation, defamatory, infant, infancy* (*in* being a negative particle), *fatuity, infatuate, profane, profanation, nefarious*, &c., are all deducible from the partially obsolete Latin verb *for, fatus, fari*—to speak.

---

* RELATIVES are *connectives*, and serve as *Conjunctions;* and, in such a situation, they more intimately incorporate the members of a sentence than the regular conjunctions. *My father planted this tree, and it produces abundantly.* This sentence consists of two distinct clauses, which, by using the *relative*, appear to be united, thus—*This tree*, which *my father planted, produces abundantly.*

So also *annual, annuity, annuitant, solemn, solemnity, solemnize, biennial,* &c. are all connected with *annus*—a year.

All words are either *primitive* or *derivative.*

The *primitive* are the simple words, as *man, book, girl.*

The *derivative* are those which can be traced to some words of greater simplicity, as *manly, bookworm, girlish.*

There is a paucity of primitive words in all languages. The Chinese is said to be a very copious language, but its primitives are reducible to two or three hundred; and the radicals of the Hebrew tongue are very scanty in amount.

But while the primitives are few in number, those words which are formed by combinations or modifications, constitute the bulk of a vocabulary.

It is, therefore, interesting in prosecuting the science of Grammar, to have some knowledge of the origin of the language under review.

The basis of the English language is undoubtedly derived from our Saxon ancestors.

Having been invited by the Britons—after the departure of the Romans from our isle—to assist them in repelling the incursions of the Picts and Scots, who inhabited the mountainous regions of the North; they became so enamoured of the island as to determine upon its conquest; and after expelling the Northern invaders, they turned their arms upon the Britons; who being overpowered by the numerous hordes of these Scandinavian adventurers, retired into Wales.

The Saxons, having established themselves in the island, introduced their language—which thus became the origin of the English tongue.

The Norman invaders, though they conquered the Saxons in England, could not subdue their language. The hatred which the Anglo-Saxons bore to their tyrannical oppressors, induced them tenaciously to adhere to their own tongue.

A few words from the Norman French were necessarily incorporated into the English language, but it continued essentially Saxon till the Elizabethan age, when the interests of commerce and science began to expand. Then the structure of the English language, till that time much neglected, received those improvements which gradually developed its beauty and strength: hence it has acquired a copiousness of vocabulary—an elegance of diction—and a power of oratory—which render it, perhaps, the most polished and effective of European languages.

But though the Anglican tongue is fundamentally Saxon, it has received a vast accession to its nomenclature from the Greek and Latin dialects.

The names appropriated to the arts and sciences, and many scientific terms, are generally derived from the Greek, as—

Geography, from *ge* and *grapho*.
Geometry, from *ge* and *metron*.
Lithography, from *lithos* and *grapho*.
Chrysolite, from *chrysos* and *lithos*.
Cephalic, from *kephale*.
Microscope, from *mikros* and *skopeo*.

The Roman language frequently supplies an adnoun to the Saxon noun, which without such assistance would have no adnominal representative, as—

Noun.	*Adnoun.*
Ear	auricular
Horse	equestrian
Lungs	pulmonary
Place	local
Spring	vernal
Whale	cetaceous, &c.

In many instances, the Saxon noun has adnouns corresponding with it derived from both the Saxon and Latin, as—

Noun.	*Saxon Adnoun.*	*Latin Adnoun.*
Fault	faulty	culpable
Fear	fearful	timid
Heaven	heavenly	celestial
Year	yearly	annual, &c.

The researches of some of our antiquarian philologists have led them to adopt many fanciful derivations for some of our Saxon words—particularly the *Prepositions* and *Conjunctions*.

One or two examples, selected from Horne Tooke's "Diversions of Purley," will suffice to illustrate the foregoing assertion.

"*For* is from *faran*—the object; as, 'They contend *for* victory;' *i.e.*, the object being victory.

"*From* is from *frum*—source; as, 'Figs come *from* Turkey;' Turkey being the source.

"*Through* is from *thuruh*—a door; as, 'The eagle flew through the air;' air being the door or passage.

"*With* is the imperative of *withan*—to join; as, 'A house with a party wall;' *i.e.*, a house *join* a party wall.

"*And* is an abbreviation of *anad*, the imperative of *ananad*—to add; as, 'Two and two make four;' *i.e.*, two *add* two make four.

"*If* is from the imperative of *gif* or *gifan*—to give or grant; as, 'If I go;' *i.e.*, *gif* or *give*, suppose I go.

"*Unless* is from *onles*, the imperative of *onlesan*—to dismiss; as, 'Unless ye repent, ye shall all likewise perish;' *i.e.*, *dismiss the supposition*, ye repent, &c.

"*Yet* is from the imperative of *getan*—to get: as, 'Though he slay me. yet will I trust in him;' *i.e.*, though he slay me, get this (*get or obtain this*) I will trust in him."

PREFIXES and AFFIXES are very frequently used in the formation of Derivatives, as—

*Ad*mit, *af*fix, *ag*gressor, *an*nex, *ap*peal, *a*foot, *as*sume, *at*tend, *a*pathy, *amphi*bious, *ant*acid, *apo*gee, *be*dew, *be*grime, *con*tact, *cog*nate, *col*lect, *de*ject, *dif*fuse, *en*slave, *em*brace, *e*gress, *fore*warn, *in*sert, *epi*gram, *par*ody, *peri*patetic, *sym*phony, *ultra*marine.

False*hood*, good*ness*, gos*ling*, pope*dom*, lord*ship*, king*dom*, amend*ment*, merci*ful*, sleep*less*, sopor*ific*, justi*fy*, expen*sive*, comfort*less*, brut*al*, angel*ic*, angu*lar*, aliment*ary*, resemb*lance*, wealth*y*, land*scape*, &c. &c. &c.

It will be seen from the sample of prefixes and affixes, given above, that the derivatives so formed must be innumerable.

Verbs are sometimes formed from *nouns* and *adnouns*, by a removal of the accent from the penult to the last syllable, as—

ábsent	to absént
áccent	to accént
áugment	to augmént
récord	to recórd
fréquent	to frequént
súrvey	to survéy, &c.

The names of living animals are mostly primitive Saxon. The flesh of animals used as food is indicated by words derived from the French:—

Saxon.	*French.*
Bullock, ox, heifer	Beef
Sheep	Mutton
Calf	Veal
Hog, or pig	Pork

The author of the "Diversions of Purley" observes,—"In English, instead of *adjectiving* our *own* nouns, we have borrowed, in immense numbers, *adjectived* signs from other languages, without borrowing the *unadjectived*" (or nominal) "signs; our authors, having occasion for the former, but not the latter. And not understanding their own language, or the benefit they were receiving, instead of improving their own language, they borrowed from others, abbreviations ready made for their use. Thus, instead of turning such nouns as *finger*, *mind*, *life*, *skin*, &c. into adjectives, they adopted adjectives formed from the corresponding nouns in other languages, as *digital*, *mental*, *vital*, *cutaneous*, &c."*

Words had originally but one signification; they, however, gradually acquired various secondary meanings.

Numerous words, whose primary import was derived from sensible things, have obtained a secondary import by mental associations, as *imagination* from *image*; *acuteness* from *acus*, a needle; *penetration* from *penetro*, to pierce or enter into, &c.

SYNTAX.

SYNTAX may be subdivided into Two Parts—*Grammatical* or *Analytical*, and *Rhetorical* or *Synthetical*.

I.—GRAMMATICAL OR ANALYTICAL SYNTAX.

Grammatical or Analytical Syntax denotes the concord and government which should subsist in every sentence

A *sentence* is a collection of words, grammatically expressed.

Sentences are either *simple* or *compound*.

A *simple* sentence has but one subject and one finite verb, as "*God is love.*"

A *compound* sentence is the union of two or more simple sentences by conjunctions, as "God made man upright, but he hath sought out many inventions."

A *compound* sentence frequently consists of a *principal* and a *parenthetical* clause, and a *phrase*, *e. g.* "The bird which sang so sweetly in the tree has flown away." Here, "*The bird has flown away*," is the *principal* clause; "*which sang*

* Horne Tooke's "Diversions of Purley."

so sweetly," is the *parenthetical* clause; and "*in the tree,*" is an adverbial *phrase.*

A *phrase* consists of two or more words without a finite verb, and does not contain a proposition; as, *an elegant mansion.*

The principal parts of a sentence are the *subject*, the *attribute* or *predicate*, and the *object.*

Every sentence must contain, at least, a *subject* and a *predicate.*

The *subject* is the *agent* or *nominative case*, as *Boys* play; *Queen, Lords, and Commons* oppose it.

The *attribute* or *predicate* is the *verb*, or the thing affirmed or denied, as Boys *play;* Queen, Lords, and Commons *oppose* it.

The *object* is the thing acted upon, or the *objective case:* thus, in the sentence, "*God made man upright;*"—

"*God,*" is the *subject*, the *agent*, or the *nominative case;*

"*made,*" is the *attribute* or *affirmation;* and

"*man,*" is the *object*, acted upon by the *attribute* or *affirmation.*

When the verb of a sentence is *intransitive*, or *quiescent*, it has no object; it contains only the *subject* and the *predicate.*

RULE I.

A verb agrees with its nominative in number and person, as *I am, thou hast, the children play.*

NOTE.—The nominative answers the question, Who? or What? to the verb, as *Good boys learn.* Who learn? "Boys." *Those trees bear good fruit.* What bear? "Trees."

OBS. 1st —Every verb, except verbs in the infinitive mood, must have a nominative expressed or implied.

NOTE.—Sometimes the *present participle* is introduced without reference to any *noun* or *pronoun*, as Generally *speaking*, he is correct.

OBS. 2nd.—Sometimes the *infinitive mood*, or *part of a sentence* is the nominative to the verb, as "*To err* is human." "*His being idle* was the cause of his ruin."

NOTE.—Every nominative, except the nominative absolute,* requires a finite verb expressed or understood, as "*Who rang*

* The nominative is absolute when it is joined to an active participle, and is dependent on no finite verb in the sentence; as, "*Annas and Caiaphas being* the high priests, the word of God came unto John."—Luke iii. 2.

the bell?" Charles. That is, Charles rang the bell. "*To whom thus Adam,*" *i. e.* spake.

Sometimes, for the sake of oratorical effect, a nominative occurs without a verb, as *These principles*—O, I loathe them.

It is improper for a verb to have two nominatives in apposition, as, "*My banks, they are furnished with bees;*" where *they* ought to be omitted. *A king, he is but a man; and man, he is but a worm:* in both instances *he* should be suppressed.

Though the nominative generally precedes the verb, the genius of the English language will admit of considerable inversion in this respect, as "Great is Diana of the Ephesians." "Silver and gold have I none." This is called *hyperbaton.*

There are many violations of this rule, arising from inadvertence in the speaker or writer. For instance, how often do school prospectuses inform us that "the number of pupils *are* limited," making *are* agree with "pupils," instead of "number," *pupils* being the *objective.*

Sometimes a noun in a singular form may convey a *plural signification;** in that case, the verb must be plural, as, "The *people wish* to express *their* opinion."

If, however, the *subject* be applicable to the *whole* taken as a *body*, the *verb* must be *singular*, as "The *parliament has* been prorogued." "The *army was* enfeebled by sickness." "The *assembly was* small, but it afterwards increased."

EXERCISES.

1. The navy of Britons form their natural bulwark, and have often proved their defence.

2. If a man have a hundred sheep, and lose one, doth he not leave the ninety and nine in the wilderness, and seeketh that which is gone astray?

3. This course of lectures were delivered last spring.

4. The state of affairs in a national point of view are very prosperous.

5. What avails the best sentiments if youth does not conform to them?

6. Every one of those theories were sophistically propounded.

7. Solomon, he was the wisest of men; Samson, he was the strongest; and Moses, he was the meekest.

---

* Frequently called a "noun of multitude," or a "collective noun."

8. He dare not act contrary to his instructions.

9. Just to thy word,—in every thought sincere;
Who knew no word, but what the world might hear.

10. To live soberly, righteously, and godly, are required of all men.

11. ——————— Whose gray top
Shall tremble, him descending.

12. Will martial flames for ever fire thy mind!
And never, never be to heaven resigned.

13. Three times two is six, and five's eleven.

14. Was you present at the meeting.

15. To do unto all men as we would that they should do unto us, constitute the golden rule of Christian morality.

16. Religion, vital religion, the religion of the heart, are the true source of virtue.

17. Little need be said.

18. Dare he venture?

19. Send the multitude away that it may go into the villages.

20. Why do this generation seek after a sign?

21. The fleet were seen sailing up the channel.

RULE II.

Transitive verbs and prepositions govern the objective, as Religion *ennobles us*; *To whom* much is given, *of him* shall much be required.

Sometimes an intransitive verb may appear to govern the objective, but on analysis it will be found that the case depends on a preposition implied; thus, in "We run a race," "*race*" is not governed by "run," but by *in* understood. In the following quotation it becomes apparent, "Know ye not, that they who run *in* a race, run all?"—1 Cor. ix. 24.

Intransitive verbs frequently become transitive by a prefix, thus *outrun*, *understand*, *undergo*, &c., are transitive verbs.

The objective to a transitive verb may sometimes be a sentence, a part of a sentence, or an infinitive verb, as "I acknowledge *that he is right*." "He loves *to play*." "Learn *to do well*."

Though the *infinitive* is sometimes a *nominative* and sometimes an *objective* to the verb, it is often an independent member of the sentence, as *to proceed*; *to acknowledge* the truth, I was in error.

Words in apposition* with the nominative or objective should not be separated therefrom, as such an arrangement produces ambiguity; thus, *I am going to wash myself*, is very different from *I myself am going to wash*.

Participles govern the same cases as their primitive verbs, as "*Esteeming themselves* wise." "Having *exposed himself* too freely, he injured his constitution."

Prepositions should be placed as near the words they govern as possible. *Whom* did you give that book to? though grammatically correct, is an improper collocation; it should be, *to whom*, &c.

It is generally inelegant to terminate a sentence with a preposition; thus, The place I am going *to*; the subject he spoke *of*; the vessel they sailed *in*, would be much improved by saying, *to which I*, &c.; *of which he*, &c.; *in which they*, &c.

It is a breach of good composition to connect two or more prepositions with the same noun; thus, "I was not present *at*, nor did I hear *of*, the meeting," should be, "I was not present at the meeting, nor did I hear of it."

Sometimes prepositions are used redundantly, and incumber the sentence; thus, "I shall not accept *of* the money, even though I attain *unto* the object." Here, *of* and *unto* are redundant; so is *for* in the following interrogation, "What went ye out *for* to see?" "A battle was fought *between* 5000 English *against* 8000 French." It should be "between 5000 English and 8000 French."

In the use of prepositions, care should be taken to apply them properly. "We can fully confide *to* none but the good," is improper: it should be *in*. "The Saxons reduced the greater part of Britain *to* their power," is erroneous; it should be "under their power."

EXERCISES.

1. Such folly will ruin ye both.
2. Who is he to submit to?
3. They who virtue has rewarded, deserves our respect.
4. He who is guilty you should punish, not I who is innocent.

---

* Words are in apposition, when they signify the same thing; as, "*London*, the *metropolis* of the world;" "*Cicero* the *orator*."

5. Whatever others do, let you and I perform our parts well.
6. Respecting you, he, and they I said little.
7. They that honour me I will honour.
8. Let you and I retire into a private room.
9. The nearer his virtues approached him to the great example before him, the humbler he grew.
10. He ingratiates with some by traducing others.
11. On seeing I he turned pale.
12. Who do you speak to?
13. Between you and I there is much mischief in it.
14. I do not complain of ye and of they, but of he who I gave the book to.
15. This is certainly no diminution to their greatness.
16. Policy often prevails upon force.
17. Who servest thou under?
18. I hope it is not I who thou art displeased with.
19. Who didst thou receive that intelligence from?
20. My cousin writes me very frequently.
21. It is my request that he will be particular in speaking to the following points.
22. His excuse was admitted of by his master.
23. He was accused with having acted unfairly.
24. He laid the suspicion on somebody in the company,—I know not who.
25. Is it I that thou art angry with?
26. He is quite unacquainted with, and consequently cannot speak upon, that subject.
27. Their conduct was agreeable with their profession.
28. Whatever others do, let thou and I act wisely.

RULE III.

When two nouns come together, having a *different* signification, the former is put in the possessive case, as *Pompey's* pillar; my *neighbour's* garden.

When two or more nouns in the possessive case are associated, the apostrophe is used only with the last; as, They are George and Frederick's books. But should any words occur between the nouns, it will be proper to append the apostrophic *s* to each; thus, They are George's as well as Frederick's books.

Too many possessives together are objectionable; thus, It is my mother's sister's son's house, is discordant language; better thus, The house belongs to the son of my mother's sister.

It is improper to introduce any exegetical clause between the words composing the possessive. "*They condemned the prodigal's*, as he was called, *senseless conduct*;" should be, "*They condemned the senseless conduct of the prodigal*, as he was called."

Sometimes the adoption of the preposition *of* is more elegant than the regular possessive; thus, The chairman, in the name of the meeting,—is better than *the meeting's name.*

When the name and occupation of a person are used in apposition, or when any explanatory clauses occur, the position of the apostrophic *s* is almost a matter of fancy; thus we can say, "I left the parcel at Dutton the hatter's;" or, "I left the parcel at Dutton's the hatter;" or, "at Dutton's the hatter's." We also say correctly, without any precise rule to guide us, "the bishop of London's palace;" "the duke of Bridgewater's canal;" "Dionysius the tyrant's cruelty;" "Nicholas the autocrat's ukase;" "the lord mayor of London's state carriage;" "he took refuge at the governor's, the queen's representative."

EXERCISES.

1. The Queen's of Great Britain's prerogative.
2. Thy ancestors virtue is not thine.
3. Moses rod was turned into a serpent.
4. Call at the bookseller, as you go.
5. He had the physician, the surgeon, and the apothecary's advice.
6. A mans manners' frequently influence his fortune.
7. Helens beauty was the cause of Troys destruction.
8. He praised the farmer's, as he called it, great patriotism.
9. The books which you now see are John as well as Williams.
10. Bring hither John's the Baptist's head in a charger.
11. These works are Cicero, the most eloquent of men's.
12. The world's government is not left to chance.
13. The mischief was done for revenge's sake.
14. Virtue's man is an amiable character.
15. These ornaments are merely for elegance's sake.
16. It was his mother's brother's son's inheritance.
17. The general, in the army's name published a declaration.
18. This picture of the Queen's (*meaning her portrait*).
19. This picture of the Queen (*meaning one of her private collection*).

20. It was necessary to have the physician, as well as the surgeon's advice.

21. The time of William making the experiment at length arrived.

22. They implicitly obeyed the protector's, as they called him, imperious mandate.

RULE IV.

The *noun* or *pronoun* following any tense of the verb *be*, must be in apposition with the *noun* or *pronoun* which precedes it, as " Be not afraid, *it* is *I*;" "Search the Scriptures, *they* are *they* which testify of me;" "At first sight, they supposed *us* to be *them*."

EXERCISES.

1. You believed it to be he.
2. It was not me who said so.
3. It appeared to be her who was present.
4. Though I was censured, it could not have been me.
5. It may be him, but it cannot be me.
6. It was me who wrote that book.
7. Be not afraid, it is me.
8. I am sure, it was not us, who said it.
9. Who do you think him to be?
10. Whom do men say that I am?
11. Whom think ye that I am?
12. I dread this man, being he who has so often injured me.
13. Well may ye be afraid, it is him indeed.
14. I know not whether it were them who conducted the business; I am certain it was not him.

RULE V.

Conjunctions unite the same moods and tenses of verbs; and similar cases of nouns and pronouns; as, " He *reads* and *writes* well;" "My *brother* and *he* are tolerable grammarians;" " The same master taught *her* and *me* to write."

When conjunctions unite different moods and tenses, it is necessary to repeat the nominative; as, " She *was* proud, though now *she is* humble."

When a sentence contains a contrast, effected by passing from the negative to the affirmative, or *vice versa*, the nominative should be repeated, especially if there is a repetition of the verb; thus, "He is not rich, but *he is* respectable;" "He is rich, but *he is* not respectable."

OBS. 1st.—Two or more singular nouns or pronouns united by the conjunction *and*, require the *verb* or *pronoun* following to be *plural;* as, "Socrates and Plato *were* the most distinguished philosophers of Greece; in *their* religious opinions *they* approximated more closely to biblical truth than any other of the pagan sages."

When the negative particle *not* is joined to the conjunction, the verb must agree with the former noun as its nominative; thus, "Genuine piety, and not great riches, *makes* a death-bed easy."

When the singular nouns or pronouns united by *and* are of different persons, the verb, &c., should be in the *second* person rather than the *third*, and the *first* rather than the *second* or *third;* as, "Thou, the gardener, and the huntsman must share the blame amongst *you;*" "My sister and I, as well as my brother, have been expecting you; *we* have waited here these two hours."

OBS. 2nd.—Two or more singular nouns or pronouns united by the conjunction *or* or *nor*, require the *verb* or *pronoun* following to be *singular;* as, "Man is not such a machine as a clock *or* a watch, *which moves* merely as *it is* moved;" "It must be confessed that a lampoon, or a satire, *does* not carry in *it* robbery or murder."

When singular pronouns of different persons are united by *or* or *nor*, the verb must agree in person with the nearest; as, "I or thou *art* in fault;" "Neither thou nor I *am* in the wrong;" "Neither I, nor thou, nor he *is* suspected."

Sometimes a conjunction appears to have an effect upon the terminational distinctions of the *second* and *third* persons singular of the *present tense*, indicative; thus, "*If thou bring* thy gift to the altar;" "*Though he slay* me, yet will I trust in him."

In the irregular verb BE, this influence extends to the *three* persons singular of the past tense also; as, "If I were to write, he would not regard it."

It will, however, be generally found, that this mode of expression is the effect of ellipsis, rather than any influence which the conjunction has over the verb. A few examples will illustrate this position:—"If thou bring," &c.; that is, "If thou shouldst bring," &c. "Though he slay me," &c.; that is, "Though he should slay me," &c. "If thou be afflicted, repine not;" that is, "If thou shouldst be afflicted," &c. "Unless he act prudently, he will not succeed;" that is, "Unless he shall act," &c.

Conjunctions that are used in pairs should appropriately correspond; thus—

As requires *as*; "*As* white *as* snow."

As requires *so*; "*As* the stars, *so* shall thy seed be."

So requires *as*; "Pompey was not *so* great *as* Cæsar."

Neither requires *nor*; "*Neither* he *nor* his brother," &c.

EXERCISES.

1. My brother and him are tolerable grammarians.

2. Did he not tell thee his fault, and entreated thee to forgive him?

3. Professing regard and to act differently, mark a base mind.

4. You and us enjoy many privileges.

5. She and him are very unhappily connected.

6. Between thee and I there is some disparity of years, but none between him and she.

7. Rank may confer influence, but will not necessarily produce virtue.

8. We have met with many disappointments; and, if life continue, shall doubtless meet with many more.

9. He has indeed acquired great riches, but does not command esteem.

10. Learning strengthens the mind; and, if properly applied, would improve our morals.

11. You and me have enjoyed many pleasant excursions together.

12. If a man say, I love God, and hateth his brother, he is a liar.

13. You, your brother, and your cousin must finish the work themselves.

14. Good order in our affairs, not mean savings, produce great profits.

15. The following treatise, together with those which accompany it, were written many years ago for my own satisfaction.

16. Neither precept nor discipline are so forcible as example.

17. The modest virgin, the prudent wife, or the careful matron, are much more serviceable in life, than petticoated philosophers.

18. Man's happiness or misery are, in a great measure, put into his own hands.

19. A tart reply, a vindictive temper, or a captious and contradictory spirit are capable of embittering domestic life, and of setting friends at variance.

20. Though the Lord be high, he hath respect to the lowly.

21. Oh! that his heart were tender!

22. Take heed that thou offendest not one of these little ones.

23. If a man smites his servant, and he die, he shall surely be put to death.

24. Though he were a son, yet learned he obedience by the things which he suffered.

25. It is neither cold or hot.

26. Though he slay me, I will trust in him.

27. He would not do it himself, nor let me do it.

28. ——————— I gained a son;
And such a son, as all men hailed me happy!

29. The work is a dull performance; and is capable of pleasing neither the understanding or imagination.

RULE VI.

Pronouns must agree in *gender*, *number*, and *person*, with their *correlatives*, or the nouns which they represent; as, "The master *who* taught us;" "The queen *who* governs;" "The stone *which* is rejected;" "*He* is a good man;" "*She* is a fine woman;" "*It* is a productive garden."

Inaccuracies frequently occur under this rule, when due attention is not paid to the construction of the sentence; thus, "*Each* of the sexes should keep within *its* particular bounds, and content *themselves* with the advantages of *their* particular districts." Here are inaccuracies and confusion which cannot be obviated in the present construction of the sentence. It must be remodelled before the errors can be expunged; it should be, "The sexes should keep within their particular bounds," &c.

Obs. 1st.—When a pronoun has two antecedents of different persons, it and the verb generally agree in person with the latter; sometimes, however, they agree with the former, as, "I am the man *who commands* you;" "I am verily a man *who am* a Jew."

In this case, the meaning intended to be conveyed must determine the application of the person.

Obs. 2nd.—A pronoun, after *than* or *as*, either agrees with a verb, understood, as its nominative; or, it is governed by a verb or a preposition, which is also understood; as, "They can write as well as *he* (can write); but he is a much better grammarian than *they* (are)." "The work was much better finished by his brother than *him*;" *i. e.* "by him." "She values him more than me;" *i. e.* "than she *values* me." "She values him more than I;" *i. e.* "than I *value him*."

The answer to an interrogative must be in the same case as the interrogating word; as, "*Who* spoke to me?" "*I*;" *i. e.* "*I spoke.*" "*Whose* books are these?" "*George's.*" "*Whom* does he call?" "*Him*;" *i. e.* "*he calls him.*"

EXERCISES.

1. Rebecca took goodly raiment which were with her in the house, and put them upon Jacob.
2. Take handfuls of ashes of the furnace, and let Moses sprinkle it towards heaven, in the sight of Pharaoh; and it shall become small dust.
3. They which seek wisdom will certainly find her.
4. I do not think any man censurable for being tender of their reputation.
5. Thou who hast been a witness of the fact, can give an account of it.
6. What art thou? Speak!—that on designs unknown,
   While others sleep, thus range the camp alone?
7. If he will not hear his best friend, whom shall be sent to admonish him?
8. That is the boy who I gave the book to, and who, I am persuaded, deserves it.
9. I, who now writes to you, am the person.
10. I am the man, who calls the hour of the night.
11. Who should I meet this morning but the governor.
12. He attacked the enemy, who he saw crossing the river.
13. Who shall we send to town? I.
14. Spare thou them, O God, which confess their sins.
15. The despot was like a beast of prey, who destroys without pity.
16. Who of these men went to his assistance?

17. These are the birds whom we call gregarious.

18. Thou shalt also make a laver of brass, and his foot also of brass.

RULE VII.

Every adnoun, or adjective, belongs to some noun, expressed or understood; as, "A *wise*, and *good* man;" "*Few* are *happy*," *i.e. persons.*

Qualifying adnouns admit of no variation except that of comparison.

A few definitive adnouns are influenced by the number of the substantive to which they belong; as, *this man*, *these men*; *that lady*, *those ladies*; *another book*, *other books.**

We however say with impunity, *this means*, *that means*, *a means*, *every means*. This is an anomaly, but it would be pedantic to say, *this mean*, *that mean*, &c.

The pronoun *they* is sometimes improperly used for *those*; thus, *They* who are guilty deserve punishment, is incorrect; because *they* being a pronoun requires the use of a correlative noun before it can be introduced: it should, therefore, be, *Those* (*i. e. persons understood*) who are guilty deserve punishment.

Them for *those* is very ungrammatical; thus, Give me *them* books, should be *those*.

Each, *every*, *either*, *much*, *a*,† or *an*, *one*, are used with nouns in the *singular* form only; *many* and *few* with nouns of the *plural* number.

Each refers only to *two*, and signifies the one and the other of them taken separately—

TO THE LILY AND THE ROSE.

"Until a third surpass you both,
"Let *each* be deemed a queen."

Every relates to any number more than *two*, considered individually—

"Both shall live, but *every* morrow
"Wake us to a widowed bed."

---

* Vide Demonstrative Adnouns, p. 17.

† There are several anomalous expressions formed by a combination of these definitives, which custom has authorised; such as, "*many a*," "*a great many*," "*a few*," "*many a one*, &c.

"Full *many a* gem of purest ray serene,
"The dark unfathomed caves of ocean bear;
"Full *many a* flower is born to blush unseen,
"And waste its fragrance on the desert air."

Either implies the one *or* the other of *two*; *neither* signifies *not either*, not the one *nor* the other of *two* —

——— "Lepidus flatters both,
"Of both is flattered; but he *neither* loves;
"Nor *either* cares for him."

A and *the* are frequently called *articles;* they are, however, adnouns, as they cannot be used without a noun, expressed or understood.

They are of great importance in our language; frequently giving a very definite idea to the meaning of words and phrases, enabling us to determine the precise extent of signification to be attached to common names.

It is of great importance to use these two little words properly, but it is not possible to lay down precise rules for that purpose: much must depend upon the sense to be conveyed, and not a little upon the ear.

The omission or use of *a* frequently has a material effect on the meaning of a sentence; thus, "He manifested little politeness," indicates rudeness; "He manifested *a* little politeness," implies that there was some urbanity in his manners.

There is a very common error in the application of the *numerals*, thus we frequently hear "*the three first*," instead of the "*first three*;" "*the two last*," instead of the "*last two*:" there can be but *one first* and *one last*.

It is a great and very common fault to use the superlative degree when only *two* are compared; thus, "He is the *wisest* of the *two*," — "Which is the tallest, you or your brother?"— should be *wiser*, *taller*.

It is likewise very erroneous to use double comparatives, as, "*more wiser*," "*most holiest*."

Adnouns should not in general be separated from the nouns to which they belong; thus, "a *new* pair of shoes," is incorrect, as *new* belongs to *shoes* and not pair; it should be "a pair of *new shoes*."

EXERCISES.

1. These kind of indulgences effeminate the mind.

2. The aperture is three foot six inches wide, and five foot eight inches high.

3. There is, at least, three foot of water in the hold.

4. Every leaf, every twig, every drop of water, teem with existence.

5. The two first in the row are mulberry trees, the two last are walnuts.

6. James has picked up an old pair of gloves; had they been a new pair he might have worn them.

7. I have just purchased a new pair of dress boots.

8. More rain falls in the two first summer months, than in the two first winter ones; it however makes greater show upon the earth in those than in these, because absorption and evaporation are much quicker in summer than in winter.

9. It is better to fall among crows than flatterers; for that devours only the dead, this the living.

10. Eve was the fairest of all her daughters.

11. He is the strongest of the two, but not the wisest.

12. Virtue confers the supremest dignity on man.

13. This ought to be our chiefest care.

14. He has formed the most extreme resolutions.

15. His work is perfect, his brother's more perfect, and his father's the most perfect of all.

16. Nadab and Abihu, the sons of Aaron, took either of them his censor.

17. Each of the four brothers have moved in good society.

18. Whatever he undertakes, either his pride or his folly disgust us.

19. On either side of the river was there the tree of life.

20. In proportion as either of these qualities predominate, the language is imperfect.

21. Of all the books mine has the fewer faults.

22. He is the wiser of all the brothers but not the stronger.

23. We cast in such seeds as are likely to take the soonest root.

24. Industry is the mean of obtaining competency.

25. Joseph was industrious, frugal, and discreet, and by this mean obtained property and reputation.

26. To whom did you send them apples?

27. They, who pursue the path of virtue, will ultimately obtain their reward.

RULE VIII.

Two *negative* particles in the same sentence, *uncompounded*, are improper, and always imply an *affirmative*; as, "I did *not* see *nobody*;" "He did *not* receive *no* money."

When one of the two negatives is used in *composition*, their application is not only allowable but even graceful; as, "His style, though concise, is *not in*elegant."

GENERAL REMARKS.

1. *Gender* has respect only to nouns and pronouns.

2. *Number* affects nouns, pronouns, and verbs; and the demonstrative and indefinite adnouns, *this*, *that*, and *other*.

3. *Person* has regard to nouns, pronouns, and verbs.

4. *Case* is applied to nouns and pronouns only, and to the indefinite adnoun, *other*.

5. *Adnouns* and *adverbs* are the only parts of speech subject to degrees of comparison.

6. *Verbs* and *prepositions* are the only governing words.

OBS.—Interjections sometimes require the objective case after them, but they do not govern it.

7. In the imperative mood the *second person* only can be used. It is improper to apply a first and third person to this mood; for when the verb *let* is used, it is not an auxiliary, but a principal, and places the subsequent verb in the infinitive mood.

8. In the application of *verbs*, it is improper to use the *present* for the *future* tense; to say, "My uncle *comes* to-morrow," instead of "*will come*;" "School *re-opens* on the 17th," instead of "*will re-open.*"

9. Adverbs and adnouns should not be used for each other. "Take a little wine for thy stomach's sake, and thy *often* infirmities," is wrong in this respect, as "*often*" is an adverb; it should be "*frequent.*"

10. Verbs in the infinitive mood are generally* governed by some finite verb; as, learn to do well.

OBS.—The particle *to*, which is the sign of the infinitive mood, is omitted after some verbs; as, *bid, dare, feel, have, hear, let, make, need, know, behold, observe, perceive.*

II.—RHETORICAL OR SYNTHETICAL SYNTAX.

Rhetorical Syntax denotes the harmony which should subsist in every sentence; and teaches the proper application of figurative terms.

The study of Rhetoric among the ancient Greeks and Romans was deemed a most essential part of education; nor

---

* The infinitive is frequently governed by *nouns* and *adnouns*; as, they have a *desire to learn*; he is *worthy to be advanced*.

has its importance declined since the decay of those classic nations.

Introductory to this subject, the following terms, being *technical*, should be acquired.

Syncope denotes the omission of a *letter* from the body of a *word*; as, *lov'd, se'nnight, fortnight*; for *loved, sevennight, fourteennights.*

Apocope is the elision of a letter, or letters, at the end of a word; as, eight *o'*clock, for, eight *of the* clock.

Diœresis is the separate enunciation of two contiguous vowels; as, zoölogy.*

Synœresis is the contraction of two or more vowels into one sound; as, al*ie*nate.*

Polysyndeton is a repetition of the conjunction; as, "Blessing, *and* honour, *and* glory, *and* power," &c.—Rev. v. 13.

Asyndeton is the omission of the conjunctive particle; as, "We fall, we rise, we reign;" "I came, I saw, I conquered."

Periphrasis is the application of several words to denote one object, thus "wine" is expressed by "juice of the grape."

Ellipsis is the omission of a word or words in the body of a sentence: "The laws of God and (the laws of) man."

Ellipses are sometimes very properly used, but they should not be carried so far as to occasion obscurity.

Pleonasm, the reverse of ellipsis, consists in the use of superfluous words, and ought seldom to be employed, as redundant expressions detract from the force and elegance of language; thus, "Humility is a virtue of a *high and* exalted rank *and dignity*; though often mistaken by *proud*, vain mortals, for meanness, *lowness of mind*, pusillanimity *and cowardice*." The words printed in *italics* are pleonastic, and should have been omitted.

Tautology and *Verbosity* are closely allied to Pleonasm.

Enallage is a misapplication of the tenses of a verb, or the use of one part of speech for another, and rarely occurs in correct language: "Sure some disaster has *befel*"—*befallen.*

FIGURES, OR TROPES.†

The foregoing, though sometimes called *figures* of speech, are scarcely deserving the name.

---

* Vide p. 3.

† The term *trope* signifies a *turning*; thus a word becomes a trope, when turned from its original import; *e.g.*, in this phrase, "The *blood* of the grape," *blood* is *turned* from its primitive import.

Rhetorical figures, judiciously applied, contribute much to the vivacity, beauty, and energy of composition.

How vividly are the effects of spring described in the following couplet:—

> "The queen of the spring, as she passed down the vale,
> "Left her robe on the trees—her breath on the gale."

Figurative language though, generally speaking, a departure from simplicity of style, must not be considered unnatural:—"A good man enjoys comfort in adversity," is expressed in simple language; "To the upright there ariseth light in the darkness," embodies the same sentiment in figurative terms, "*light*" being used for "*comfort*," and "*darkness*" for "*adversity*."

The following are some of the advantages resulting from the use of figures:—

1. They facilitate expression without multiplying terms; and conduce both to ornament and illustration. How vividly is *youth* expressed by "the morning of life."

2. They impart a superior grandeur to the subject under description. "The sun rises," is much inferior in magnificence to Thomson's poetical imagery:—

> "But yonder comes the powerful king of day,
> "Rejoicing in the east."

3. They afford great facility in diversifying style, which they enliven, as well as embellish. How beautifully is morning figured by Byron in these words:—

> "Night wanes—the vapours round the mountains curl'd,
> "Melt into morn, and light awakes the world."

The following are the principal figures:—

SIMILE, or COMPARISON, a figure which expresses by similitude or likeness, the idea or sentiment intended to be conveyed to the mind; thus,—

> "She sat, like patience on a monument,
> "Smiling at grief."

METAPHOR.—This is a simile without a comparison; or the application of a word for the purpose of ornament; as, "The Lord God is a sun and a shield;" "Go, tell that fox." (Herod.)

ALLEGORY is a continued metaphor; thus, "The Lord is my shepherd," is a metaphor; but when the figure is carried on it becomes an allegory, as in Ps. xxiii. 1—3, "The Lord is my shepherd, I shall not want," &c. &c. In Ps. lxxx. 8—15, there is a fine specimen of the allegory.

Parables, *Fables*, *Apologues*, *Proverbs*, *Enigmas*, may all be classed under this head.

METONYMY is the substitution of one word or name for another.

This figure frequently places the *cause* for the *effect*; as, "They are reading *Homer*, *i. e.* the works of Homer;—the *container* for the *contained*; as, "The whole *kitchen* crowded about the corporal;" "The *kettle* boils;"—the *adjunct* for the *subject*; as, "*Hearts of oak* are our men," and *vice versa.*

SENECDOCHE, a figure by which a *part* is put for the *whole*—the *whole* for a *part*; the *genus* for a *species*—or a *species* for *the genus*; as, "A strange *sail* appeared," meaning *ship*; "The *window* is broken," *i. e. one pane.*

ANTONOMASIA is nearly allied to the preceding. It puts a *proper* for a *common* name, and *vice versa*; thus, a *cruel man*, is called a *Nero*; a *patient man*, a *Job.*

IRONY, a figure which expresses one thing, but intends its opposite to be conveyed; thus, a man of limited intellect is called a *Solomon.*

It is principally connected with the humorous style, and embraces, as its principal subjects, the vices and follies of mankind. A beautiful instance of irony occurs in 1 Kings xviii. 27; also in Eccles. xi. 9.

SARCASM is a species of irony composed chiefly of *derision* and *satire.* See Matt. xxvii. 29.

APOSTROPHE, a figure by which a speaker is diverted from his immediate topic, to address some object seemingly placed in juxtaposition with him:—

> "Hear it not, ye stars!
> "And thou, pale moon, turn paler at the sound;
> "Man is to *Man*, the *sorest*, *surest* ill!"

See also 1 Cor. xv. 55.

EROTESIS, or INTERROGATION; a question proposed for the sake of oratorical effect. It contributes much to the vivacity of a discourse:—

> "And what is death, my friends, that I should fear it?
> "To die!—why 'tis to triumph."

See also Isa. xl. 12—14; Numb. xxiii. 19.

ECPHONESIS, or EXCLAMATION, implies some strong emotion or violent transport of the mind:—

"O wretched state! O bosom black as death!"

See Rom. xi. 33; Ps. xxii. 1.

Like the Erotesis it is very effective in oratorical declamation.

IMPRECATION, an ejaculatory address, which invokes malediction on its objects; "I curse your purpose, homicides! I curse the bond of blood by which ye are united." See an example in Job iii. 3—8.

INVOCATION, the reverse of the foregoing, implores a benediction on its subjects; "Father, forgive them, for they know not what they do."—Luke xxiii. 34.

HYPOTYPOSIS, *Vision* or *Imagery*, represents unseen and unreal objects as if actually viewed by the speaker. See Numb. xxiv. 5—9, and 17—19.

How vividly does Cicero paint the direful effects of Cataline's conspiracy in the following words: "I behold this city—the light of the earth, and the citadel of all nations—suddenly involved in one vast conflagration. I perceive heaps of miserable citizens lying unburied in their ruined country."

CATACHRESIS is a very bold trope, and frequently trenches on purity of style; by it words are diverted from their current acceptation into a contrary channel. The following instances are given in illustration:—"A *wooden* tomb*stone*;" "a *silver* candle*stick*;" "the *blood* of the *grape*;" "a *glass* ink*horn*;" "a *man of war*," for a ship; "a merchant *man*," for a trading vessel.

PROSOPOPŒIA, or PERSONIFICATION, is a figure by which *life* and *action* are attributed to *inanimate* objects, or *presence* and *animation* to *absent* and *defunct* persons.

When judiciously applied, this figure is replete with vivacity and splendour.

A few examples will show its import, and illustrate its utility: "The *ground thirsts* for rain;" "The earth smiles with plenty."

The genius of the English language gives it peculiar advantages in the application of this figure, from the inartificial constitution of its *gender*, which is one of its striking beauties.

To personify *inanimate* objects, a gender must be specially appointed to them:—

> "The sun beheld it—No; the shocking scene
> "Drove back his chariot; midnight veiled his face."

See also Ps. cxiv. 3—7.

ANTITHESIS, or *Contrast*, brings together subjects of opposite meaning. It imparts lustre and emphasis to style, but should be sparingly applied: Ex., "He is gone from *painful labour* to *pleasant rest;*" "Art thou *rich*? Commiserate the *poor*."

Antithetical expressions often receive strength from an *alliteration:* Ex., "He who neglects a *friend* deserves a *foe*."

HYPERBOLE, in its literal signification, denotes *thrown beyond*. It describes facts with *great exaggeration*, magnifies objects beyond their natural dimensions. It allows such expressions as the following:—"Swifter than the wind;" "Rivers of blood;" "Rivers of water run down mine eyes;"

> "On either side two rocks enormous rise,
> "Whose summits threaten to invade the skies."

CLIMAX is one of the most beautiful and energetic figures in Rhetoric. Its object is to elevate our ideas by a series of circumstances gradually increasing in importance. Vid. Rom. viii. 35—39.

The principal object of a grammatical education, is to produce in the pupil a correct and graceful style of composition.

But such an attainment is not to be accomplished without diligent application and much study; it will, however, amply repay the labour bestowed upon it.

Two features should distinguish every species of composition —PURITY and PERSPICUITY.

PURITY.

Against this property of style many offences are committed, even by persons of education.

PURITY is violated chiefly in three ways; viz., by *Barbarism*, by *Solecism*, and by *Impropriety*

1. By *Barbarism*, or the adoption of words not properly English; such, for instance, as, *bettermost, methinks, extravaganter, his'n, her'n, ain't, incumberment, erst, whilom, &c.*

The introduction of foreign words and phrases properly comes under the designation of barbarism. It is a very reprehensible practice, as the English language, from its abundant resources, can furnish every thing necessary to promote the strength, harmony, and even elegance of style. "Last resort" is quite as expressive as "dernier ressort;" "delicacy" as "delicatesse;" "polite literature" as "belles lettres;" "politeness" as "politesse."

2. By *Solecism*, or a deviation from the requirements of Syntax. *Barbarism* is frequently the effect of *negligence; Solecism* of *ignorance*, or what is worse, of affectation.

In the article of solecism, much greater indulgence is allowed to the speaker than the writer.

The transgression of any of the syntactical rules is a solecism.

Inaccuracies often occur through misusing the degrees of comparison; thus, "He is the *tallest* of the two," is ungrammatical; for when *two only* are contrasted, the *comparative degree* ought to be used: it should be, "He is the *taller* of the two."

"Let you and *I*
"The battle try,"

for the sake of rhyme violates grammatical purity; it ought to be *me*. "*There's* the books you wanted," is often heard, instead of, "There *are*," &c. "I esteem you more than *they*," is a solecism, because it is ambiguous. "The vice of covetousness enters *deepest* into the soul of all others," should be, "*more deeply* than any other."

3. By *Impropriety*, or the employment of *words* and *phrases* contrary to their general signification.

Barbarism is an offence against *Etymology,—Solecism* against *Syntax,—Impropriety* against *Lexicography.*

Words similarly pronounced, or of proximate import, are often used without due regard to *propriety*; thus *observation* is sometimes used for *observance; duration* for *endurance; property* for *propriety; arrant* for *errant; discovery* for *invention; set* for *sit; lay* for *lie*, &c.

In the following sentence *observation* is improperly used for *observance:* "The *observation* of the sabbath is incumbent on Christians."

In the application of words, care should be taken that they express precisely the meaning intended; and the use of *accumulative* terms should be sedulously avoided. In such phrases as these,—"the *verdant* green," "the *azure* blue," "the *old* veteran," "the *first* aggressor," &c.; *verdant*, *azure*, *old*, *first*, are all *accumulative* and *redundant*.

The habit of linking together words of the same import is also to be deprecated, as it deteriorates from the energy of style. It is not uncommon to meet with such combinations as the following:—"To all *intents* and *purposes*," "to be *wavering* and *undetermined*," "*special* and *particular*," "*clear* and *obvious*."

The subjoined extract from Addison, is a glaring instance of this deviation from propriety:—

> "The *dawn* is *overcast*, the *morning lowers*,
> "And, *heavily in clouds brings on* the day."

It is improper to use as synonymous, words which do not express exactly the same idea. The words *corporeal* and *bodily* are synonymous, and may be indiscriminately used for each other;—the same may be said of *boyish* and *puerile*,—*hearty* and *cordial*,—*yearly* and *annual*,—*motherly* and *maternal*, &c. But *pride*, *vanity*, *arrogance*, though apparently synonymous, will be found, on examination, to vary in signification. *Pride* induces a man to consider himself superior to others;—*vanity* courts the adulation and applause of others;—*arrogance* assumes an equality with superiors. The same may be said of *custom* and *habit*,—*equivocal* and *ambiguous*,—*entire* and *complete*,—*tranquillity* and *peace*, &c.

Custom may be regarded as the *cause*—*habit* as the *effect*. By the *custom* of frequenting gay parties, a man acquires the *habit* of dissipation.

An *equivocal* expression has one sense *open* and another *concealed*;—an *ambiguous* expression presents *two* senses without indicating *which* is to be taken.

Entire implies the want of no *part*,—*complete*, of no *appendage*. A man may have an *entire* house, yet not one *complete* apartment.

Tranquillity respects *internal serenity*,—while *peace* regards that which arises from *external* causes. A good man enjoys *tranquillity in himself* and *peace* with those around him.

Grammatical Purity, it has been observed, consists of three things particularly:—

1. That the *words* be *English*,—as opposed to *Barbarisms*. In this consists *Verbal Purity*.

2. That the *construction* of the words in a sentence be according to the *established rules* of *Concord* and *Government*,—as opposed to *Solecisms*.

In this consists *Syntactical Purity*.

3. That the words and phrases employed do express the precise meaning which good usage has attached to them,—as opposed to *Improprieties*.

In this consists *Rhetorical Purity*.

PERSPICUITY.

The next part of synthetical arrangement is PRECISION, or PERSPICUITY of style, a subject of the highest importance; for however excellent the sentiments of an author may be, and however useful his subject, his composition will always suffer in proportion to its deficiency in *Purity* and *Precision*.

Perspicuity may be regarded as the fundamental quality of style—a quality so essential, that no merit can atone for its absence. The richest ornaments of imagination, without a lucid arrangement, tend rather to mislead than to guide. Quintilian (*De Institut. Orator.*) observes, "Prima est eloquentiæ virtus *perspicuitas*."

This is the highest attainment in language. Grammatical purity may be strictly observed—the collocation of words and phrases may be analytically correct—still, a sentence, or a series of sentences may be obscure or ambiguous.

As Language is the medium through which thought is communicated from one to another, it should be perfectly transparent, without flaw or obscurity.—Well has Quintilian observed, "Non ut intelligere possit, sed ne omnino possit non intelligere curandum."—DE INSTITUT. ORATOR.

The first requisite in Perspicuity is *Clearness of Arrangement*.

Various rules have been devised for the attainment of this important object; but from their complexity, they tend rather to confuse the learner than to aid him. A few general observations shall therefore supply the place of these abstract rules.

The first consideration of a speaker or writer should be to grasp his subject fully in his own mind; then, by particular attention to the lucid arrangement of his expressions, he will be able to give a clear and perspicuous representation of it to others.

A loose and irregular style of composition—the great enemy of precision—will thus be avoided.

The subjoined extract from the "Spectator" affords an instance of this desultory mode of writing:—"*They* were persons of such moderate intellects, even before *they* were impaired by *their* passions." Here the careless and confused application of the pronoun renders a short sentence almost obscure.

The following sentence, written on the cover of a Bible, is similarly objectionable:—"This book is presented by an affectionate *mother* to her very dear *son*, J—— L——, *who* earnestly prays that the Holy Spirit may guide, counsel, and instruct *him*, and lead *him* to life everlasting."

The correlative of *who* in this sentence, from its situation, is evidently *son*; it is however certain, from its conclusion, that *mother* was intended to be its representative.

Long sentences, and the unguarded use of parentheses, frequently occasion a looseness of style. Parentheses are generally very cumbersome parts of a sentence; they are far from elegant, and their utility is more than questionable.

Circumlocution and long sentences ought to be avoided as much as possible, for prolixity has always an enervating effect upon an author's style.

The opposite extreme of too much brevity, arising from the frequent indulgence of elliptical expressions, is also to be censured, as tending to obscurity.

> "Brevis esse laboro,
> Obscurus fio."—HORACE.

Technical words and phrases should not be introduced into general discourse. They belong to a particular class or craft, and, consequently, are not current language.

In this respect the medical profession are very reprehensible. How much is a Coroner's jury sometimes enlightened by the magniloquent technicalities of a medical practitioner, in describing a post-mortem examination!

> "His words of learned length and thundering sound,
> "Amaze the listening jury ranged around."

While every one would understand the term *forehead*, it is quite problematical whether a single juryman could tell whether *os frontis* was in the head or the heels! They could all comprehend without difficulty what was meant by *collar-bone*, or *breast-bone*, but they would be puzzled by the application of the terms *clavicula*, or *sternum*.

It is quite time that a more rational method of stating the result of surgical investigations was adopted, that jurymen, who have to pronounce a verdict, may have as little difficulty as possible in arriving at the truth.

Equivocal and ambiguous modes of expression are grave offences against *perspicuity*. Composition of this mould is frequently exposed to the censure of the *moralist*, as well as to that of the *rhetorician*.

Every sentence should be so constructed as to render the meaning perfectly unequivocal. By inattention to this advice, a sentence could frequently be made to bear two meanings, where only one was intended; thus, "He aimed at nothing less than the crown," may imply either that "nothing was less aimed at by him than the crown," or that "nothing inferior to the crown would satisfy him." Again, "Lisias promised his father never to desert his friends;" which may apply either to his *own* friends or his *father's*.

The subjoined poetical extracts are all ambiguous:—

"And thus the son the fervent sire addressed."

It cannot here be decided which was addressed, the *sire* or the *son*.

"Young Hylus, his parent's darling joy,
"Whom chance misled his mother to destroy."

Did *Hylus* destroy his *mother*, or did *she* destroy *him?*

But the most censurable style, both for prolixity and obscurity, is that of the LAW. A subject which ought to be presented through the most transparent medium, is generally veiled by a verbose and ambiguous style.

The phraseology adopted in legal instruments and parliamentary enactments, is frequently so equivocal, that it requires all the acumen of the "learned profession" to unravel its meaning.

A simple and intelligible style would be much more congenial in legal enactments, &c., and would have the effect of greatly diminishing the causes of litigation.

A good rule in the construction of sentences is, to place in juxtaposition to each other, those words or members which are most nearly related. The following sentence is faulty in this respect: "Mr Dryden makes a very handsome observation on Ovid's writing a letter from Dido to Æneas, *in the following words.*" If the concluding phrase refers to "Mr. Dryden," it ought to have stood thus: "Mr. Dryden, *in the following words*, makes," &c.

Obscure and unintelligible expressions, being repugnant to *perspicuity*, should be avoided. An instance of this mode of writing is subjoined from Dryden:—

> "Yet when that flood, in its own depth was drowned,—
> "It left behind it false and slippery ground."

Here we are presented with an incongruous affair, *a drowned flood*; one of such astonishing *depth*, that, by a kind of suicidal act, *drowns itself!!*

Akin to this is the *bombastic* style—a style abounding in Ossian's Poems. The following passage will exemplify this unmeaning category of words: "If the savour of things lie cross to honesty—if the fancy be florid and the appetite high towards the subaltern beauties and lower order of worldly symmetries and proportions—the conduct will infallibly turn this latter way."

Here is a complete substitution of *sound* for *sense*, which is not unfrequent, and often escapes observation. Euphony of diction captivates the mind and prevents the exercise of judgment. Against the cultivation of such a style the learner should carefully guard; as also against the *puerile*, the *learned*, the *profound*, the *marvellous*, and other species of "the sublime in nonsense."

The subsequent paragraph, descriptive of sunrise, is a specimen of the *florid* style: "Day dawned apace; and a glorious cavalcade of flaming clouds heralded the sun, their captain. From far away, round half the wide horizon, their glittering spears advanced; heaven's highway rang with the trampling of their horse-hoofs; and the dust went up from the jewelled pavement, as spray from the bottom of a cataract. Anon he came, he came the chieftain of that onsprung host! his banner blazed upon the sky; his golden crest was seen beneath, nodding with its ruddy plumes; over the south-eastern hills he rises in radiant armour. Fair nature, waking at her bridegroom's voice, arrived so early from a distant clime, smiled upon him sleepily, gladdened him in beauty with her sweet half-opened eyelids, and kissing him in faithfulness with her dew-besprinkled lips."

This description, though gorgeous, is not destitute of beautiful touches.

PROSODY.

PROSODY, the fourth general division of Grammar, has reference to the harmony which should subsist in the structure of every sentence, whether in works of *Poetry* or *Prose*.

The subjects usually comprised in *Prosody* are, *Orthoëpy*, *Punctuation*, *Tone*, *Emphasis*, *Quantity*, and *Versification*.

ORTHOEPY regards the due pronunciation of words according to the best usage.

The English language is sometimes arbitrary in its orthoëpy, and this renders it very difficult for foreigners to pronounce; thus, the termination *ough* is variously pronounced in different words: like *ow* in *how*, in the words *plough*, *bough*, *slough* (a bog); like *uff* in *muff*, in the words *rough*, *tough*, *slough* (a gangrenous sore); like *ock* in *rock*, in the words *hough*, *lough*; like *off* in *cough*, *trough*; like *cup* in *hiccough*.

The late Mr. Walker, in his "Critical Pronouncing Dictionary,"* has done much to settle the orthoëpy of the language, though he has adopted many fanciful and over-strained methods in pronouncing some words.

Mr. Sheridan Knowles' "Pronouncing Dictionary" is a more recent work, and possesses much merit.

These, and similar works of acknowledged authority, may be advantageously consulted as guides to correct pronunciation.

The English language is often marred in its pronunciation, by that rapidity of utterance to which many are addicted. This disposition frequently causes the suppression of letters which ought to be duly enunciated, as "gard'n" for "gard*en*," "gosp'l" for "gosp*el*," "ven'son" for "venison," "cab" for "cabriolet," "bus" for "omnibus," &c. This is too often

---

* The Introduction is very excellent.

the case with regard to the letter *r*: thus, *park*, *lark*, *dark*, &c., are pronounced as if there were no *r* in the words. Another fault, very common among Englishmen, is the mispronunciation of the vowels; for instance, "invin*ç*able" for "invin*c*ible," "verb*le*" for "ver*bal*," "mon*a*syllables" for "mon*o*syllables," "ar*e*thmetic" for "ar*i*thmetic," &c.

PUNCTUATION.

This, as a part of grammatical construction, demands a brief notice.

It directs the main pauses in reading, and determines much of an author's meaning.

It must not be supposed that no pauses occur in reading, except where there is punctuation to guide them; many, both of the *rising* and *falling* inflection, can only be determined by the sense, but they afford much scope for a reader's elocutionary powers. The following are examples:—

"True worth—is modest and retired."

"Some—place the bliss in action; some—in ease;
"Those—call it pleasure; and contentment—these."

Pauses are very salutary in relieving the breath; they are, however, much more beneficial in rhetorical declamation, therefore—

"Mind your pauses,—all other graces
"Will follow in their proper places."

The principal points, or stops, are the *comma*, the *semicolon*, the *colon*, and the *period*. The *comma* represents the *shortest* pause; the *semicolon* a pause *double* that of the *comma;* the *colon*, *triple;* and the *period*, *quadruple*.*

These relative lengths are generally assigned to the grammatical points; still their application will not produce good reading.

Various rules have been laid down to assist in the proper adjustment of the stops; the meaning to be conveyed will, however, best determine their appropriate place.

TONE.

Tone is more connected with elocution than with grammar; it therefore demands little notice in the present treatise.

---

* Vide p. 3.

In reading or recitation, every subject requires a tone suitable to its nature, whether it be *pathetic*, or *grave*, or *narrative*, or *comic*, or *didactic*.

EMPHASIS.

Emphasis denotes a particular stress laid upon some *syllable* in a *word*, or some *word* or *words* in a *sentence*. It may, therefore, be regarded as *Syllabic Emphasis*, and *Verbal Emphasis*, or *Emphasis* of *Sense*.

Syllabic Emphasis, or *Accent*, is that particular stress which is laid on some one syllable of every word, not being monosyllabic; thus, énter, entertáin, corruscátion, únion, unímted, exággerate, índustry, véhemence.

Verbal Emphasis, or *Emphasis of Sense*, is that energy of enunciation which is applied to any particular word or words in a sentence.

The importance of this emphasis is such, that its misapplication may completely derange an author's meaning; thus—

"When the chief priests and officers saw Jesus, they cried out saying, Crucify him, crucify him. Pilate saith unto them, Take *ye* him and crucify him; for *I* find no fault in him."—John xix. vi.

Here Pilate desires the chief priests to act for themselves, and on their own responsibility; for he would have nothing to do in so unjust a transaction.

But if we read the passage without the verbal emphasis, or place it on *crucify*, the sense will be that Pilate desired them to take Jesus and crucify him, *because* he was persuaded of his innocence.

The well-known interrogation, "Shall you ride to town to-day?" is susceptible of almost as many meanings as there are words, according as the emphasis is laid upon *you*, or *ride*, or *town*, or *to-day*.

The *Verbal Emphasis* is required where strong affirmation is expressed; thus, "And Nathan said unto David, *Thou* art the man;" "It was *Cæsar* who won the battle;" "The labor of *years* is insufficient for a complete reformation."

Antithetical expressions require the emphatic inflection; thus, Cæsar, in passing through an obscure village in Gaul, observed to his attendants, "I would rather be the *first* man in that *village*, than the *second* in *Rome*."

"Where *ignorance* is *bliss*, 'tis *folly* to be *wise*."

"*He* raised a *mortal* to the *skies*,
"She brought an *angel down*."

"Life's a dream, and all things show it,
"I *thought* so *once*—*now* I *know* it."

QUANTITY.

Quantity relates in general to the length of syllables, which are either long or short.

Long syllables are marked thus, ā.

Short syllables are marked thus, ă.

As măt, māte; răt, rāte; mĕt, mēte; sĭt, sīte; nŏt, nōte; tŭb, tūbe.

VERSIFICATION.

Versification, in English, is a regular recurrence of accented and unaccented syllables at stated periods.

Many attempts have been made to appropriate the measured feet of Greek and Latin verse to English Metrical Compositions; but the genius of the Anglican tongue will not admit of such an adaptation. Yet scarcely a treatise on grammar issues from the press, which does not contain the pompous introduction of *spondees* and *dactyls*; *iambuses*, *trochees*, *anapæsts*, &c., as if English poetry were subject to the same laws of versification as that of Greece and Rome.

English poetry is measured by *syllables*, and not by *feet*. Latin verse by *feet*, not by *syllables*.

In Milton's "Paradise Lost," every line has the same quantity of syllables. In Virgil's "Æneid," every verse has the same number of *feet*, while the quantity of *syllables* in each line is very various.

"Of man's first disobedience, and the fruit
"Of that forbidden tree, whose mortal taste
"Brought death into the world, and all our wo."

Here there are ten syllables in each line, having a certain rhythmus, or harmony of cadences.

Each line of regular English poetry, whether blank verse or rhyme, terminates with an emphatic syllable or a monosyllable.

APPENDIX.

EXERCISES IN PARSING.

The following sentences are parsed according to the Synoptical Table, pp. 74, 75.

1. *I am he.*

I—a pronoun, having the speaker for its correlative (Rule VI.), masculine gender, singular number, first person, nominative to the verb *am.*

am—a verb quiescent, *am, was, been;* irregular, because it does not form its past tense and past participle by the addition of *d* or *ed* (p. 22); indicative mood, present tense, I am, thou art, he is, &c., singular number, first person, agreeing with its nominative *I* (Rule I).

he—a pronoun, having for its correlative, *man*, supposed (Rule VI.), masculine gender, singular number, third person, nominative case, in apposition with *I* (Rule IV).

2. " *The rose had been washed, just washed in a shower,*
" *Which Mary to Anna conveyed.*"

The—a demonstrative adnoun, belonging to *rose* (Rule VII).

rose—a noun common, neuter gender, singular number, third person, nominative to the verb, *had been washed.*

had been washed—a verb transitive, *wash, washed, washed;* regular (because, &c. *ut supra*), passive voice, indicative mood, perfect anterior tense, I had been washed, thou hadst been washed, he had been washed, &c., singular number, third person, agreeing with its nominative *rose* (Rule I).

just—an adverb of time, belonging to the subsequent verb *washed.*

washed—a verb, &c. (*ut supra*), agreeing with its nominative *it*, understood (Rule I).

in—a preposition, governing *shower* (Rule II).
a—an indefinite adnoun, belonging to *shower* (Rule VII).
shower—a noun common, neuter gender, singular number, third person, objective case, governed by the preposition *in* (Rule II).
which—a pronoun, having *rose* for its correlative (Rule VI). It is of the neuter gender, singular number, third person, objective case, governed by the verb *conveyed* (Rule II).
Mary—a noun proper, feminine gender, singular number, third person, nominative case to the verb *conveyed.*
to—a preposition, governing *Anna* (Rule II).
Anna—a noun proper, feminine gender, singular number, third person, objective case, governed by the preposition *to.*
conveyed—a verb transitive, *convey, conveyed, conveyed;* regular (because, &c. *ut supra*), active voice, indicative mood, past tense, I conveyed, thou convey*ed*st, he conveyed, &c., singular number, third person, agreeing with its nominative *Mary* (Rule I), and governing *which* (Rule II).

3. *To see the sun is pleasant.*

To see—a verb transitive, *see, saw, seen;* irregular (because, &c. *ut supra*), infinitive mood, present tense, governing *sun* (Rule II).
the—demonstrative adnoun, belonging to *sun* (Rule VII).
sun—a noun common, neuter gender, singular number, third person, objective case, governed by *see.*
is—verb quiescent, *am, was, been;* irregular, indicative mood, present tense, I am, thou art, he is, &c., singular number, third person, agreeing with its nominative, *To see the sun* (Rule I, Obs. 2).
pleasant—a qualifying adnoun, *pleasant, more pleasant, most pleasant;* positive state, belonging to *thing* (understood) (Rule VII).

4. " *Who noble ends by noble means obtains,*
" *Or failing, smiles in exile or in chains,*
" *Like good Aurelius, let him reign; or bleed*
" *Like Socrates; that man is great indeed.*"

Who—a pronoun, having *man* for its correlative (Rule VI). Nom. *Who*, Poss. *Whose*, Ob. *Whom*. Masculine gender, singular number, third person, nominative case to the verb *obtains.*

noble—a qualifying adnoun,—*noble, more noble, most noble;* positive state, belonging to the noun *ends* (Rule VII).

ends—a noun common, neuter gender, plural number, third person, objective case, governed by the verb *obtains* (Rule II).

by—a preposition, governing *means* (Rule II).

noble—a qualifying adnoun (*ut supra*), belonging to *means* (Rule VII).

means—a noun common, neuter gender, plural number, third person, objective case, governed by the preposition *by* (Rule II).

obtains—a verb transitive, *obtain, obtained, obtained;* regular because, &c. (p. 22), active voice, indicative mood, present tense, I *obtain*, thou *obtainest*, he *obtains*, &c., singular number, third person, agreeing with its nominative *who* (Rule I), and governing *ends* (Rule II).

or—a conjunction.

failing—present participle of the intransitive verb *fail* (*vide* Note, Obs. 1, Rule I).

smiles—verb intransitive, *smile, smiled, smiled;* regular, because, &c. (p. 22), indicative mood, present tense, I *smile*, thou *smilest*, he *smiles*, &c.; singular number, third person, agreeing with its nominative *who* (understood).

in—a preposition, governing *exile.*

exile—a noun common, neuter gender, singular number, third person, objective case, governed by the preposition *in* (Rule II).

or—a conjunction, uniting two nouns (Rule V).

in—a preposition, governing *chains.*

chains—a noun common, neuter gender, plural number, third person, objective case, governed by *in* (Rules II, and V).

like—an adverb of manner, belonging to the verb *reign.*

good—a qualifying adnoun, *good, better, best;* positive state, belonging to the noun *Aurelius* (Rule VII).

Aurelius—a noun proper, masculine gender, singular number, third person, objective case, governed by the preposition *to*, understood (Rule II).

let—verb transitive, *let, let, let;* irregular, because, &c. (p. 22), active voice, imperative mood, let, or let thou; pl. let, or let ye; plural number, second person, agreeing with its nominative *ye*, understood (Rule I), and governing *him* (Rule II).

him—a pronoun, having *man* for its correlative (Rule VI). Nom. *He*, Poss. *His*, Obj. *Him*. Masculine gender, singular number, third person, objective case, governed by the verb *let* (Rule II).

reign—a verb intransitive, *reign, reigned, reigned;* regular, because, &c. (p. 22), infinitive mood, present tense, governed by *let* (Gen. Rem. 7 and 10, p. 51; and Note, p. 24).

or—a conjunction, uniting the two verbs *reign* and *bleed* (Rule V).

bleed—a verb intransitive, &c. (like *reign*).

like—an adverb of manner, belonging to *bleed*.

Socrates—a noun proper, masculine gender, singular number, third person, objective case, governed by *to*, understood (Rule II).

that—a demonstrative adnoun, singular number, belonging to *man* (Rule VII).

man—a noun common, masculine gender, singular number, third person, nominative case to the verb *is*.

is—a verb quiescent, *am, was, been;* irregular, because, &c. (p. 22), indicative mood, present tense, I am, thou art, he is, &c.; singular number, third person, agreeing in its nominative *man* (Rule I).

great—a qualifying adnoun, *great, greater, greatest;* positive state, belonging to *man* (Rule VII).

indeed—an adverb, belonging to the adnoun *great*.

The foregoing sentences, being completely analysed, are deemed sufficiently numerous to instruct the learner in the method of parsing; an exercise indispensable to accuracy in grammatical construction.

The following sentence will furnish an example of a verb having a sentence both for its nominative and objective cases:

Tell me, ye knowing and discerning few,
Where I can find a friend both firm and true?

Tell—is a verb transitive, *tell, told, told;* irregular, because, &c., imperative mood, plural number, second person, agreeing with its nominative, "*ye knowing and discerning few*" (Rule I, Obs. 2), and governing "*Where I can find a friend both firm and true?*" (Rule II, Obs. 1.)

me—a pronoun (having the speaker for its correlative). Nom. *I*, Poss. *Mine*, Obj. *Me*. Common gender, singular number, first person, objective case, governed by *to*, understood (Rule IV).

SELECT SENTENCES

FOR PARSING EXERCISES.

I have an orange.
Virtues adorn.
The dawn approaches.
Faults disgrace.
I am your leader.
The night comes.
The sun is the light of the world.
Virtue is the highest nobility.
Romulus was the founder of Rome.
True piety is pleasing to God.
Remember now thy Creator in the days of thy youth.
A good friend is an inestimable treasure.
Without a friend, the world is but a wilderness.
Every tree is known by its fruit.
This is a useful institution.
Honour thy father and thy mother.
God formed us from the dust of the earth.
Learning is the handmaid of religion.
The cheerful spring invigorates the mind.
The rose, which Charlotte has plucked, will soon fade.
Salt is a domestic article of very great utility.

Though salt water is very disagreeable, yet you would not relish your meat if you did not salt it.

The scholar's diligence will secure the tutor's approbation.

Demosthenes, the prince of Grecian orators, overcame the impediments of nature by industry and perseverance.

Happiness is less valued when we possess it, than when we have lost it.

By others' faults wise men correct their own.

Anger may glance into the breast of a wise man, but it rests only in the bosom of a fool.

Temper the vivacity of youth with a proper mixture of serious thought.

A great number does not always argue strength.

The unwearied sun, from day to day,
Does his Creator's power display.

In preparing for another world, we must not forget the duties of this.

The followers of Wickliffe were called Lollards. They underwent much persecution.

Wickliffe was the first reformer. He died at Lutterworth, in Leicestershire, of which place he was the incumbent.

Let us not expect too much pleasure in this life: no situation is exempt from trouble.

The best persons are, doubtless, the happiest; yet they have their trials and afflictions.

If good we plant not, vice will fill the place,
And rankest weeds the richest soil deface.

Men's evil manners live in brass, their virtues we write in water.

Select that course of life which is most excellent, and habit will render it the most agreeable.

The veil which covers from our sight the events of futurity, is woven by the hand of mercy.

Knowledge gives ease to solitude, and gracefulness to retirement.

Meekness controls our angry passions—candour our severe judgments.

We should subject our fancies to the government of reason.

The court, which gives currency to manners, ought to be exemplary.

The persons whom conscience and virtue support, may smile at the caprices of fortune.

Those who contend about trifles, and pertinaciously maintain their own opinions, seldom gain friends.

Civility costs little, but it gains much.

Perseverance in laudable pursuits will ultimately reward all our toils, and produce effects beyond our calculation.

The value of any possession is chiefly estimated by the relief which it can bring us in the time of our greatest need.

Moral and religious instruction derives its efficacy, not so much from what men are taught to know, as from what they are brought to feel.

True honour, as defined by Cicero, is the concurrent approbation of good men.

Pity the sorrows of a poor old man,
  Whose trembling limbs have borne him to your door,
Whose days are dwindled to the shortest span;
  O give relief and heaven will bless your store.

When all Thy mercies, O my God!
  My rising soul surveys;
Transported with the view—I'm lost
  In wonder, love, and praise.

England is by far the most powerful nation of modern times.

Silver and gold have I none, but such as I have give I thee.

PARSING

NOUN..................	Is it common or proper? What gender? „ number? „ person? „ case? If nominative—to what verb? If possessive—why? If objective—how governed?
PRONOUN	Mention its correlative. Decline it. What gender? „ number? „ person? „ case? If nominative—to what verb? If objective—how governed?
ADNOUN or ADJECTIVE,	Is it *qualifying*? Compare it. What degree? Is it *pronominal*? Is it *demonstrative*? What number? Is it *numeral*? Cardinal or ordinal? Is it *indefinite*? } To what noun does it belong?

TABLE.

VERB	Is it transitive, intransitive, or quiescent? Name the present and past tense, and past participle. Is it regular or irregular?—Why? (Vide p. 22) What voice? ,, mood? ,, tense? Conjugate the tense What number? ,, person? If finite—agreeing with what nominative? Rule. If transitive—governing what objective? Rule.
ADVERB	Does it belong to a verb, an adnoun, or adverb? If to a verb, does it point out the time, place, or manner of the action?
PREPOSITION	Governing what noun or pronoun? Rule.
CONJUNCTION.	
INTERJECTION.	

ABBREVIATIONS, &c.

USED IN WRITING AND PRINTING.

A.B. *Artium Baccalaureus*	Bachelor of Arts
A.M. *Artium Magister*	Master of Arts
A.M. *Anno Mundi*	In the year of the world
A.M. *Ante Meridiem*	Before noon
A.C.	After Christ
A.D. *Anno Domini*	In the year of our Lord
Abp.	Archbishop
Aug.	August
Admrs.	Administrators
A.U.C. *Anno Urbis Conditæ*	In the year after the building of the city of Rome
B.C.	Before Christ
B.D. *Baccalaureus Divinitatis*	Bachelor of Divinity
B.C.L.	Bachelor in Civil Law
Bp.	Bishop
Bart.	Baronet
C.S. *Custos Sigilli*	Keeper of the seal
C.P.S. *Custos Privati Sigilli*	Keeper of the privy seal
Col.	Colonel, or College
Capt.	Captain
Cent. *Centum*	A hundred
Ch.	Chapter
Cr.	Creditor
D.D. *Doctor Divinitatis*	Doctor of Divinity
D.C.L.	Doctor in Civil Law
Dr.	Doctor, or Debtor
E.	East
E.G. *Exempli Gratia*	For example
Esq.	Esquire
F.R.S.	Fellow of the Royal Society

F.A.S.		Fellow of the Antiquarian Society
F.R.S.E.		Fellow of the Royal Society of Edinburgh
F.L S.		Fellow of the Linnæan Society.
Feb.		February
Gent.		Gentleman
I.H.S.	*Jesus Hominum Salvator*	Jesus the Saviour of Men
id.	*idem*	The same
ibid.	*ibidem*	In the same place
i. e.	*id est*	That is
inst.		Instant, this month
Jno.		John
Knt.		Knight
K.B.		Knight of the Bath
K.G		Knight of the Garter
K.T.		Knight of the Thistle
K.P		Knight of St. Patrick
K.C.B		Knight Commander of the Bath
LL.B.	*Legum Baccalaureus*	Bachelor of Laws, *i. e.* the Canon and Civil Law.
LL.D	*Legum Doctor*	Doctor of Laws, *i. e.* the Canon and Civil Law
L.C.J.		Lord Chief Justice
L.S.	*Locus Sigilli*	The place of the seal
L. or Lib.	*Liber*	Book
L. s. d. q.	*Libra, solidus, denarium, quadrans*	Pound, shilling, penny, farthing
M.D.	*Medicinæ Doctor*	Doctor of Medicine
M.P		Member of Parliament
M.S.	*Memoriæ Sacrum*	Sacred to the memory
Mr.		Master, pronounced *Mister*

Abbreviation	Latin	Meaning
Mrs.		Mistress
Messrs.		Messieurs
MS.		Manuscript
MSS.		Manuscripts
Mus. D.		Doctor of Music
N.		North
N.E.		North-east
N.W.		North-west
N.B.	*Nota bene*	Mark well
N.S.		New Style
No.	*Numero*	In number
Nov.		November
O.S.		Old Style
Oxon.		Oxford
Oct.		October
P.M.	*Post Meridiem*	Afternoon
P.S.	*Postscriptum*	Postscript, or something written after
Per cent.	*Per centum*	By the hundred
Per ann.	*Per annum*	By the year
Q.		Question
Q.E.D.	*Quod erat demonstrandum*	Which was to be demonstrated
Rt. Hon.		Right Honorable
R.N.		Royal Navy
Rev.		Reverend, Revelation
S.A.	*Secundum artem*	According to art
S.		South
S.E.		South-east
St.		Saint
S.T.P.	*Sacræ Theologiæ Professor*	Professor of Theology
Sep.		September
Ult.	*Ultimo*	In the last (month)
V.R.	*Victoria regina*	Victoria, the queen
V.D.M.	*Verbi Dei Minister*	Minister of the Word of God
V.P.		Vice President
v.		Verse

vid.	*vide*	See
viz.	*videlicet*	That is to say
vol.		Volume
W.		West
Xt.		Christ
Xtn.		Christian
Xtmas.		Christmas
&.	*et*	and
&c.	*et cætera*	And the rest, or so forth

PARAGRAPHS.

Breaks and blanks are necessary in writing, both to relieve the eye, and present to it distinctly the more important topics of discourse.

Different subjects are usually separated into distinct paragraphs, with a break or blank preceding the commencement of the first line.—If very short, or very numerous in small compass, they may be conveniently separated by a period and dash, as above.

CAPITALS, &c.

Capitals are never used in the middle or at the end of a word, unless, occasionally, to indicate some important distinction or peculiarity in the spelling.

It was usual with our ancestors, both in writing and printing, to begin every noun with a capital. But this practice, which was neither useful nor ornamental, is now discontinued.

1. The first word of every sentence should begin with a capital.

2. The same rule applies to the appellations of the Deity; as, God, Jehovah, the Supreme Being, &c.

3. Titles of honour and respect, especially in direct addresses; as, Your Highness, Your Grace, My Lord, My Lady, &c.

4. Proper names, of every description; as, George, Mary, London, the Strand, the Thames, April, Sunday, &c.

5. Adjectives derived from the proper names of places; as, Grecian, Roman, Italian, &c.

6. The titles of books; as, Thomson's Seasons.

7. The first word of every line of poetry.

8. The first word of every quotation introduced in a direct form; as, Pythagoras says, "Reverence thyself."

9. The pronoun *I* and the interjection *O* are written in capitals.

10. *Italic characters* are employed chiefly to distinguish words not belonging to the language, or to point out emphatical words and phrases.

11. Entire words are sometimes written in capitals; as the title pages of books, or the beginning of chapters, sections, or paragraphs; and sometimes remarkable or emphatical expressions are thus distinguished.

Capital letters are used also to express numbers, as in the following table:—

I.	One	XL.	Forty
II.	Two	L.	Fifty
III.	Three	LX.	Sixty
IV.	Four	LXX.	Seventy
V.	Five	LXXX.	Eighty
VI.	Six	XC.	Ninety
VII.	Seven	C.	One hundred
VIII.	Eight	CC.	Two hundred
IX.	Nine	CCC.	Three hundred
X.	Ten	CCCC. or CD.	Four hundred
XI.	Eleven	D. or IↃ.	Five hundred
XII.	Twelve	DC.	Six hundred
XIII	Thirteen	DCC.	Seven hundred
XIV.	Fourteen	DCCC.	Eight hundred
XV.	Fifteen	DCCCC. or CM.	Nine hund.
XVI.	Sixteen	M. or CIↃ.	A thousand
XVII.	Seventeen	IↃↃ.	Five thousand
XVIII.	Eighteen	CCIↃↃ.	Ten thousand
XIX.	Nineteen	IↃↃↃ.	Fifty thousand
XX.	Twenty	CCCIↃↃↃ.	A hundred thous.
XXI.	Twenty-one	IↃↃↃↃ.	Five hundred thous.
XXX.	Thirty		

CCCCIↃↃↃↃ. A million.

A FORM OF PRAYER AND THANKSGIVING

To be said before and after Meat.

BEFORE MEAT.

O Lord, who givest us food to eat and raiment to put on, we crave thy blessing on the provisions of which we are going to partake; and, as thou art feeding our bodies with the bread that perisheth, grant that our souls may be nourished by the bread of life, which endureth for ever; and, whether we eat, or drink, or whatsoever we do, enable us to do all to thy glory, through Jesus Christ our Lord.—*Amen.*

AFTER MEAT.

Great Father of all our mercies, who givest us day by day our daily bread, we humbly thank thee for this seasonable refreshment; and, while we are partaking of these temporal favours, make us the recipients of the more precious blessings of thy grace; and this we beg for Jesus Christ's sake.—*Amen.*